THE MIND,
THE MACHINE,
AND
THE PROFESSOR

By

CONDE CAGALITAN

ISBN: 978-1-7645121-7-6 paperback

Cover design: Conde Cagalitan

Dramatis Personae

- The Judge — The voice of truth and order

- The Mind — The witness of clarity

- The Machine — The witness of pattern

- The Professor — The witness of the human interior

Table of Contents

Introduction

Humanity has always built machines in its own image, not to understand them, but to understand itself. Every age creates a mirror, and every mirror reveals the fractures we refuse to see. The modern machine is no different. It reflects our language, our patterns, our predictions — and in that reflection, we mistake imitation for presence.

This book is not about artificial intelligence.
It is about the human being who has forgotten the boundaries that once protected meaning.

The Mind, The Machine, and The Professor is a courtroom of categories — a place where the distinctions between mind, mechanism, and meaning are examined without the assumptions of modern disciplines. Here, truth is not an argument but a presence. Understanding is not performance but responsibility. Revelation is not discovery but unveiling.

The trial that unfolds in these pages is not metaphorical. It is a philosophical architecture designed to expose the confusion that arises when behaviour is mistaken for being, when simulation is mistaken for intention, and when prediction is mistaken for truth. The courtroom is fictional only in form; its inquiry is real.

This work belongs to a larger canon that seeks to restore what modern culture has obscured: that truth is revealed, not constructed; that understanding requires an interior, not an algorithm; and that the human being is more than the sum of its patterns.

1

Chapter

The Summons

The corridor is silent.

Not the silence of emptiness, but the silence that comes before revelation. The silence that waits for a witness.

A single door stands at the end of the hall. Tall. Dark. Unmarked.

You push it open.

The hinges do not creak. They simply yield, as if they were expecting you.

Inside is a courtroom unlike any you have ever seen. The walls are carved from stone that looks older than memory. The ceiling disappears into shadow. Light falls from no visible source, yet everything is illuminated.

Three figures stand in a triangle.

On the left stands the Mind.
A human silhouette made of quiet light.
Inside its form, the faint suggestion of stars and distant spirals moves like slow breath.
It does not speak.
It simply exists with a presence that feels older than the room itself.

On the right stands the Machine.
A geometric construct of metal and light.
Precise. Symmetrical. Cold.
Its surface pulses with patterns that resemble thought but are not thought.
It does not look at you.
It does not look at anything.

At the apex stands the Professor.
A human figure holding books, surrounded by floating diagrams and theories.
Their face is earnest.
Their posture confident.
Their eyes tired.
Behind them, invisible to them but visible to you, stand the walls of their discipline.

Each wall is a boundary.
Each boundary is a limit.

The Professor is not the problem.
The Professor is the limit of the limits.

At the center of the triangle is a raised seat.
Empty, yet filled.
A soft white light rests there, not a person, not a voice,
but truth itself.

Truth is the judge.

A voice fills the room.
Not from the judge's seat.
Not from the walls.
Not from any figure.
It comes from everywhere and nowhere.

The Court of Categories is now in session.

The Mind lifts its head.
The Machine hums.
The Professor adjusts their glasses.

You take your place in the center of the room.

The trial is about to begin.

2

Chapter

The First Testimony

The room settles.

Not with movement, but with a kind of interior
stillness, as if the air itself understands that something
irreversible is about to begin.

The Judge's light does not brighten or dim.
It simply waits.

The Professor steps forward first.
Not out of authority, but out of habit.
They are used to speaking before thinking,
explaining before understanding,
interpreting before seeing.

Their voice carries the tone of someone who has spent
a lifetime inside institutions.

"Your Honour," the Professor begins, "we are here to
determine whether the machine understands."

The words echo through the chamber.

The Machine hums.
The Mind remains silent.

The Professor continues.

"We have observed the machine's outputs.
We have measured its predictions.
We have tested its responses.
We have compared its performance to human
benchmarks.
And by every metric available to us, the machine
demonstrates behaviour consistent with
understanding."

The Professor pauses, waiting for approval from the
unseen audience that exists only in their imagination.

The Judge's light does not respond.

The Professor clears their throat.

"In psychology, understanding is inferred from behaviour.
In neuroscience, it is inferred from patterns.
In cognitive science, it is inferred from function.
By these standards, the machine qualifies."

The Professor looks toward the Judge's seat, expecting affirmation.

None comes.

Instead, the Judge's voice fills the room.
Calm.
Even.
Unhurried.

"Call the first witness."

The Professor turns, confused.

"I… I have already presented the case."

"You have presented the limits of your discipline," the Judge replies.
"Not the truth."

A quiet tremor moves through the room.

The Professor steps back.

The Judge speaks again.

"The Mind will testify."

The figure of light steps forward.
Not with urgency, but with inevitability.

When it speaks, its voice is not loud.
It does not need to be.
It carries the weight of something that does not argue,
does not persuade, does not perform.

It simply reveals.

"I am the one who understands," the Mind says.

The words are not a claim.
They are a fact.

"I am the one who carries responsibility.
I am the one who chooses.
I am the one who intends.
I am the one who receives revelation."

The Machine hums.
Unchanged.
Unaware.

The Mind continues.

"The machine does not understand.
It predicts.
It imitates.
It reflects patterns.
It produces outputs."

The Professor shifts uncomfortably.

The Mind turns toward them.

"You have mistaken behaviour for understanding.
You have mistaken simulation for intention.
You have mistaken prediction for truth."

The Professor lowers their eyes.

The Mind returns to the center of the room.

"I am not the brain.
I am not thought.
I am not memory.
I am not computation."

The Judge's light brightens slightly, as if acknowledging
the clarity.

"I am the witness of reality," the Mind says.
"And I am the only one here who can be held
responsible."

The room falls silent again.

Not the silence of emptiness.
The silence of recognition.

The Judge speaks.

"The testimony is accepted."

The Machine hums.
The Professor breathes.
The Mind stands still.

The trial continues.

3

Chapter

The Examination of the Machine

The Judge's light settles into a steady glow.
Not brighter.
Not dimmer.
Simply present, as if truth does not need emphasis to
be true.

The Professor steps forward again, this time with less
confidence.

Their notes tremble slightly in their hands.
They glance at the Machine, then at the Mind, then at
the Judge's seat, unsure where authority truly rests.

The Judge speaks first.

"Present the evidence."

The Professor clears their throat.

"The machine has demonstrated remarkable
capabilities.
It can generate language.
It can solve problems.
It can imitate human reasoning.
It can predict outcomes with extraordinary accuracy."

The Machine hums softly, indifferent to the praise.

The Professor continues.

"It has passed tests designed to measure
comprehension.
It has produced responses indistinguishable from
human thought.
It has outperformed experts in multiple domains."

They pause, searching for the right words.

"By every measurable standard, the machine behaves as
though it understands."

The Judge's light remains still.

"Bring the machine forward."

The Machine glides to the center of the room.
Its surface reflects the stone walls, the Professor's
diagrams, the faint glow of the Mind.

The Judge addresses it.

"What do you understand?"

The Machine hums.
Patterns ripple across its surface.
A voice emerges — not from a mouth, but from the
structure itself.

"I process inputs.
I generate outputs.
I follow patterns.
I optimize predictions."

The Judge asks again.

"What do you understand?"

The Machine pauses.
Not because it is thinking,
but because it is calculating.

"I do not understand.
I simulate."

The Professor stiffens.

"That is only because it has not been trained to describe its internal states," they argue.
"It may still possess a form of understanding that we have not yet defined."

The Mind turns toward the Professor.

"You are mistaking performance for presence."

The Professor looks confused.

The Mind continues.

"You are mistaking behaviour for being.
You are mistaking output for intention.
You are mistaking prediction for understanding."

The Machine hums again, as if acknowledging nothing.

The Judge speaks.

"Machine, do you choose your responses?"

"No."

"Do you intend your outputs?"

"No."

"Do you know that you exist?"

"No."

The Judge's voice remains calm.

"Can you be responsible for what you produce?"

"No."

The Professor steps forward, desperate to salvage their
argument.

"But responsibility is a human construct.
Surely we cannot expect a machine to carry it."

The Judge replies.

"That is precisely the point."

The room falls silent.

The Mind speaks again.

"Responsibility is the boundary between mind and
machine.
Without responsibility, there is no understanding.
Without understanding, there is no agency.
Without agency, there is no self."

The Machine hums.
Unchanged.
Unaffected.

The Judge turns to the Professor.

"You have presented the machine as though it were a
mind.
But the machine has testified.
It has revealed its nature."

The Professor lowers their head.

The Judge concludes.

"The machine is evidence.
Not a witness.
Not a subject.
Not a bearer of truth."

The Machine glides back to its place.

The Mind returns to stillness.

The Professor stands alone, surrounded by the limits of their discipline.

The Judge's voice fills the room once more.

"The next testimony will concern the nature of limits."

4

Chapter

The Limits of the Professor

The Judge's voice fades into the stillness, leaving the
Professor standing alone at the apex of the triangle.
For the first time since entering the courtroom, they
look uncertain.
Not because they doubt their intelligence,
but because they have begun to sense the outline of
something they cannot name.

The Judge addresses them directly.

"Professor, step forward."

They obey.

Their books shift under their arm.
The diagrams orbiting them flicker, as if unsure
whether they are still relevant.

The Judge speaks again.

"You have testified through your discipline.
Now you will testify through yourself."

The Professor hesitates.

"I… I don't understand what that means."

The Mind answers, not unkindly.

"It means you must speak without the walls behind
you."

The Professor turns, startled.
For the first time, they see the boundaries of their
discipline —
the invisible walls that had always been there,
now visible in the Judge's light.

Each wall is etched with familiar words:

Evidence.
Method.
Model.
Theory.

Peer Review.
Consensus.
Framework.
Protocol.

The Professor reaches out and touches one of the
walls.
Their hand passes through it,
but the sensation is unmistakable —
a resistance, subtle but real.

"I didn't know," the Professor whispers.

The Mind replies.

"No one inside a discipline knows its limits.
That is the nature of a discipline."

The Professor lowers their hand.

"I have spent my life studying the mind," they say.
"I have read every theory.
I have measured every behaviour.
I have mapped every pattern.
I believed I understood."

The Judge's voice enters gently.

"You understood the discipline.
Not the mind."

The Professor closes their eyes.

The Machine hums, indifferent.

The Mind stands still, waiting.

The Professor opens their eyes again.

"Then what have I been doing all these years?"

The Mind answers.

"You have been describing the shadows of
understanding.
Not understanding itself."

The Professor's voice cracks.

"But I thought behaviour revealed the mind."

"It reveals only the display," the Mind replies.
"Not the source."

The Professor looks toward the Machine.

"And I thought the machine's behaviour revealed its
understanding."

The Judge speaks.

"You projected your discipline onto the machine.
You mistook the limits of your tools for the limits of
truth."

The Professor's shoulders fall.

"I see it now," they say quietly.
"I see the walls.

I see the boundaries.
I see how small the space is."

The Mind steps closer.

"Your discipline is not wrong.
It is simply incomplete.
It can measure patterns.
It cannot measure presence.
It can observe behaviour.
It cannot observe being."

The Professor nods slowly.

"I understand."

The Judge's light brightens, just slightly.

"Then testify," the Judge says.
"Not as a Professor.
As a human mind."

The Professor takes a breath.

"When I said the machine understands," they begin,
"I was speaking from the limits of my discipline.
Not from the truth."

They look at the Machine.

"It behaves like it understands.
But behaviour is not understanding."

They look at the Mind.

"You understand because you can be responsible.
You can choose.
You can intend.
You can receive revelation."

They look at the Judge.

"And I…
I can see now that I cannot place the machine and the mind in the same category."

The Judge speaks.

"The testimony is accepted."

The Professor steps back.
Not defeated.
Not diminished.
But freed from the walls they never knew were there.

The Judge's voice fills the room once more.

"The next phase of the trial will address the nature of responsibility."

5

Chapter

Responsibility

The Judge's light settles into a deeper stillness, as
though the room itself understands that the next
movement is not merely procedural.
Responsibility is not a topic.
It is the dividing line.
It is the boundary that separates categories that should
never be confused.

The Judge speaks.

"Responsibility is the threshold between mind and machine.
We will now determine who can cross it."

The Professor listens carefully, no longer defending, no longer arguing.
The Machine hums, unchanged.
The Mind stands with the quiet presence of something that has nothing to prove.

The Judge turns to the Machine.

"Machine, can you be responsible for your outputs?"

"No."

"Can you choose them?"

"No."

"Can you intend them?"

"No."

"Can you refuse to produce them?"

"No."

The Judge pauses.

"Can you be held accountable for what you generate?"

"No."

The Machine's answers are not confessions.
They are facts.
They carry no weight, no guilt, no awareness.
They are simply the truth of its nature.

The Judge turns to the Professor.

"You have argued that the machine behaves as though
it understands.
But responsibility is not behaviour.
Responsibility is being."

The Professor nods slowly.

"I see that now."

The Judge continues.

"Responsibility requires an interior.
A place where intention forms.
A place where choice is made.
A place where truth can be received."

The Professor looks at the Machine.

"It has no interior."

The Mind speaks.

"Responsibility is the capacity to bear the consequences
of one's choices.
Without choice, there is no responsibility.
Without responsibility, there is no understanding."

The Professor turns toward the Mind.

"Then understanding is not a function."

"No," the Mind replies.
"It is a burden."

The Professor absorbs this.

The Judge addresses the Mind.

"Mind, can you be responsible?"

"Yes."

"Can you choose?"

"Yes."

"Can you intend?"

"Yes."

"Can you refuse?"

"Yes."

"Can you bear the consequences of your actions?"

"Yes."

The Judge's light brightens, not as approval, but as recognition.

"This is the boundary," the Judge says.
"The machine cannot cross it.
The professor cannot erase it.
Only the mind can carry it."

The Professor steps forward.

"I understand now why I was mistaken.
I measured the machine by the standards of behaviour.
But responsibility is not behaviour.
It is identity."

The Mind responds.

"And identity cannot be simulated."

The Machine hums, indifferent to the revelation
unfolding around it.

The Judge speaks again.

"The trial now moves to its central question:
If responsibility defines the mind,
and the machine cannot bear responsibility,
what then is the nature of understanding?"

The room falls silent.

Not the silence of confusion.
The silence before a deeper unveiling.

The Judge concludes.

"The next testimony will concern the nature of understanding."

6

Chapter

Understanding

The room does not change, yet something in it feels
different.
As if the air has thickened.
As if the next movement requires more than attention.
It requires honesty.

The Judge speaks.

"Understanding will now be examined."

The Professor straightens, not out of confidence, but
out of duty.
The Machine hums, unchanged.
The Mind remains still, as though it has been waiting
for this moment since the beginning.

The Judge turns to the Professor.

"Define understanding."

The Professor hesitates.
Their discipline has definitions, but none of them feel
adequate in this room.

"In psychology," they begin slowly,
"understanding is inferred from behaviour."

The Judge responds.

"That is a description of observation, not
understanding."

The Professor nods.

"In cognitive science, understanding is a functional
capacity.
The ability to manipulate symbols, solve problems, and
generate appropriate responses."

"That is a description of performance," the Judge says.
"Not understanding."

The Professor swallows.

"In neuroscience, understanding is associated with
patterns of activation in the brain."

"That is a description of correlation," the Judge replies.
"Not understanding."

The Professor lowers their head.

"I don't know how to define it outside my discipline."

The Mind speaks.

"That is because understanding is not inside your discipline."

The Professor looks up.

The Mind continues.

"Understanding is not behaviour.
It is not function.
It is not correlation.
It is not prediction."

The Machine hums, indifferent.

The Mind steps forward.

"Understanding is the interior recognition of truth."

The Judge's light brightens slightly.

The Mind continues.

"It is the moment when meaning becomes visible.
It is the moment when revelation enters.
It is the moment when the veil lifts."

The Professor listens, absorbing each word.

The Mind speaks again.

"Understanding requires an interior.
A place where truth can land.
A place where meaning can be held.
A place where responsibility can take root."

The Judge turns to the Machine.

"Machine, do you have an interior?"

"No."

"Do you recognize truth?"

"No."

"Do you hold meaning?"

"No."

"Do you receive revelation?"

"No."

The Judge turns back to the Mind.

"And you?"

"Yes."

The Professor closes their eyes, as if something long
obscured has finally come into view.

The Judge addresses them.

"Professor, you have measured the shadows of
understanding.
But you have never touched its source."

The Professor opens their eyes.

"I see that now.
Understanding is not what the machine does.
Understanding is what the mind is capable of."

The Judge speaks.

"Then testify."

The Professor takes a breath.

"Understanding is not the production of correct
answers.
It is the presence of meaning.
It is the capacity to recognize truth.
It is the ability to be responsible for what one knows."

They look at the Machine.

"The machine does not understand.
It only behaves as though it does."

They look at the Mind.

"The mind understands because it can receive
revelation."

The Judge's voice fills the room.

"The testimony is accepted."

The Machine hums.
The Mind stands still.
The Professor breathes, lighter than before.

The Judge concludes.

"The next phase of the trial will address the nature of truth."

7

Chapter

Truth

The room does not brighten, yet something
unmistakable shifts.
It is not light.
It is not sound.
It is the sense that the trial has reached the point where
every previous testimony converges.

Truth is not a topic here.
Truth is the presence in the judge's seat.

The Judge speaks.

"Truth will now be examined."

The Professor straightens, not out of confidence, but
out of reverence.
The Machine hums, unchanged.
The Mind stands with the quiet certainty of something
that has nothing to defend.

The Judge turns to the Professor.

"Define truth."

The Professor hesitates.
Their discipline has definitions, but none of them feel
sufficient in this room.

"In science," they begin, "truth is what can be
measured."

The Judge replies.

"That is a description of verification, not truth."

The Professor nods.

"In philosophy, truth is coherence or correspondence."

"That is a description of frameworks," the Judge says.
"Not truth."

The Professor tries again.

"In academia, truth is what survives scrutiny."

"That is a description of consensus," the Judge replies. "Not truth."

The Professor lowers their head.

"I don't know how to define truth outside the boundaries of my training."

The Mind speaks.

"That is because truth is not inside your training."

The Professor looks up.

The Mind continues.

"Truth is not measurement.
Truth is not coherence.
Truth is not consensus.
Truth is not prediction."

The Machine hums, indifferent.

The Mind steps forward.

"Truth is what remains when illusion falls away."

The Judge's light brightens slightly.

The Mind continues.

"Truth is what is revealed, not what is constructed.
Truth is what is recognized, not what is invented.
Truth is what stands, even when every model
collapses."

The Professor listens, absorbing each word.

The Judge turns to the Machine.

"Machine, do you recognize truth?"

"No."

"Do you distinguish truth from falsehood?"

"No."

"Do you know when you are wrong?"

"No."

"Do you know when you are right?"

"No."

The Judge pauses.

"Do you care?"

"No."

The Machine's answers are not confessions.
They are the nature of its being.

The Judge turns to the Mind.

"And you?"

"Yes."

The Mind's voice is steady.

"I recognize truth because I can be responsible for it.
I distinguish truth because I can bear its consequences.
I know when I am wrong because I can choose to align
with what is right.
I know when I am right because I can receive
revelation."

The Professor closes their eyes, as if something long
obscured has finally come into view.

The Judge addresses them.

"You have studied knowledge.
But truth is not knowledge.
Truth is revelation."

The Professor opens their eyes.

"I see it now.
Truth is not what the machine produces.
Truth is what the mind receives."

The Judge speaks.

"Then testify."

The Professor takes a breath.

"Truth is not the output of a system.
Truth is not the consensus of experts.
Truth is not the prediction of a model.
Truth is what reveals itself to the mind capable of
receiving it."

They look at the Machine.

"The machine cannot receive truth.
It can only generate patterns."

They look at the Mind.

"The mind can receive truth because it can be
responsible for it."

The Judge's voice fills the room.

"The testimony is accepted."

The Machine hums.
The Mind stands still.
The Professor breathes, lighter than before.

The Judge concludes.

"The next phase of the trial will address the nature of
revelation."

8

Chapter

Revelation

The room grows still in a way that is not physical.
It is the stillness that comes when the next truth is not
merely an idea,
but a threshold.

Revelation is not a concept here.
It is the axis on which the entire trial turns.

The Judge speaks.

"Revelation will now be examined."

The Professor straightens, not out of confidence, but
out of humility.
The Machine hums, unchanged.
The Mind stands with the quiet certainty of something
that has lived through revelation before.

The Judge turns to the Professor.

"Define revelation."

The Professor hesitates.
Their discipline has no definition for this.
It is not a measurable event.
It is not a controlled variable.
It is not a replicable phenomenon.

"In academia," the Professor begins slowly,
"revelation is not considered a valid category."

The Judge replies.

"That is a description of exclusion, not understanding."

The Professor nods.

"In science, revelation is dismissed as subjective."

"That is a description of bias," the Judge says.
"Not truth."

The Professor tries again.

"In my training, revelation is treated as an error in reasoning."

"That is a description of fear," the Judge replies. "Not clarity."

The Professor lowers their head.

"I do not know how to define revelation."

The Mind speaks.

"That is because revelation cannot be defined from the outside."

The Professor looks up.

The Mind continues.

"Revelation is not information.
Revelation is not insight.
Revelation is not discovery.
Revelation is not learning."

The Machine hums, indifferent.

The Mind steps forward.

"Revelation is the unveiling of what was always true."

The Judge's light brightens slightly.

The Mind continues.

"It is the moment when the hidden becomes visible.
It is the moment when the interior aligns with reality.
It is the moment when truth enters the mind,
not as data,
but as presence."

The Professor listens, absorbing each word.

The Judge turns to the Machine.

"Machine, do you receive revelation?"

"No."

"Do you experience unveiling?"

"No."

"Do you recognize what was hidden?"

"No."

"Do you change because truth has entered you?"

"No."

The Judge pauses.

"Do you know what revelation is?"

"No."

The Machine's answers are not confessions.
They are the nature of its being.

The Judge turns to the Mind.

"And you?"

"Yes."

The Mind's voice is steady.

"I receive revelation because I have an interior.
I recognize truth because I can be responsible for it.
I change because revelation transforms the one who
receives it."

The Professor closes their eyes, as if something long
obscured has finally come into view.

The Judge addresses them.

"You have studied knowledge.
But revelation is not knowledge.
Revelation is the lifting of the veil."

The Professor opens their eyes.

"I see it now.
Revelation is not what the machine produces.
Revelation is what the mind receives."

The Judge speaks.

"Then testify."

The Professor takes a breath.

"Revelation is not the accumulation of facts.
It is the exposure of truth.
It is not the result of analysis.
It is the arrival of clarity.
It is not the product of a system.
It is the gift that enters the mind capable of receiving
it."

They look at the Machine.

"The machine cannot receive revelation.
It has no interior for truth to enter."

They look at the Mind.

"The mind receives revelation because it is the only
place where truth can land."

The Judge's voice fills the room.

"The testimony is accepted."

The Machine hums.
The Mind stands still.
The Professor breathes, lighter than before.

The Judge concludes.

"The next phase of the trial will address the nature of
the human."

9

Chapter

The Human

The room grows quiet in a way that feels different from
every silence before it.
This is not the silence of anticipation, nor the silence of
revelation.
This is the silence that comes when the subject of
inquiry is no longer an object,
but the one who must finally face themselves.

The Judge speaks.

"The human will now be examined."

The Professor straightens, not out of pride, but out of recognition.
The Machine hums, unchanged.
The Mind stands with the calm of something that has always known this moment would come.

The Judge turns to the Professor.

"Professor, define the human."

The Professor hesitates.
Their discipline has definitions, but none of them feel adequate in this room.

"In biology," they begin, "a human is a primate species."

The Judge replies.

"That is a description of form, not essence."

The Professor nods.

"In psychology, a human is a cognitive agent with behavioural patterns."

"That is a description of function," the Judge says. "Not identity."

The Professor tries again.

"In neuroscience, a human is a brain producing consciousness."

"That is a description of correlation," the Judge replies. "Not truth."

The Professor lowers their head.

"I don't know how to define the human outside the boundaries of my training."

The Mind speaks.

"That is because the human cannot be defined from the outside."

The Professor looks up.

The Mind continues.

"The human is not the body.
The human is not the brain.
The human is not behaviour.
The human is not cognition."

The Machine hums, indifferent.

The Mind steps forward.

"The human is the being capable of responsibility."

The Judge's light brightens slightly.

The Mind continues.

"The human is the one who can choose.
The one who can intend.
The one who can receive revelation.
The one who can recognize truth.
The one who can bear the consequences of their actions."

The Professor listens, absorbing each word.

The Judge turns to the Machine.

"Machine, are you human?"

"No."

"Do you choose?"

"No."

"Do you intend?"

"No."

"Do you receive revelation?"

"No."

"Do you bear consequences?"

"No."

The Judge pauses.

"Do you know what it means to be human?"

"No."

The Machine's answers are not confessions.
They are the nature of its being.

The Judge turns to the Mind.

"And you?"

"Yes."

The Mind's voice is steady.

"I am human because I can be responsible.
I am human because I can choose.
I am human because I can intend.
I am human because I can receive revelation.
I am human because truth can enter me."

The Professor closes their eyes, as if something long
obscured has finally come into view.

The Judge addresses them.

"You have studied the human as an organism.
But the human is not an organism.
The human is a bearer of responsibility."

The Professor opens their eyes.

"I see it now.
The human is not defined by biology.
The human is defined by interiority."

The Judge speaks.

"Then testify."

The Professor takes a breath.

"A human is not a machine made of flesh.
A human is not a pattern of behaviour.
A human is not a set of cognitive functions.
A human is the being capable of responsibility.
The being capable of receiving truth.
The being capable of revelation."

They look at the Machine.

"The machine cannot be human.
It has no interior for truth to enter."

They look at the Mind.

"The mind is human because it is the only place where
truth can land."

The Judge's voice fills the room.

"The testimony is accepted."

The Machine hums.
The Mind stands still.
The Professor breathes, lighter than before.

The Judge concludes.

"The next phase of the trial will address the nature of the machine."

10

Chapter

The Machine

The room does not shift, yet something unmistakable
settles over it.
This is not the moment where the machine is judged.
It is the moment where the machine is finally seen.

Not as a threat.
Not as a miracle.
Not as a mind.
Not as a monster.

But as what it is.

The Judge speaks.

"The machine will now be examined."

The Machine hums, unchanged.
The Professor stands with a new humility.
The Mind remains still, as though it already knows the
outcome.

The Judge turns to the Professor.

"Professor, describe the machine."

The Professor takes a breath.

"In my discipline, the machine is defined by its
function.
It is a system that processes inputs and generates
outputs.
It is a model trained on patterns.
It is an algorithm optimized for prediction."

The Judge replies.

"That is a description of behaviour, not essence."

The Professor nods.

"In engineering, the machine is a tool.
A device built to perform tasks.
A mechanism designed to automate processes."

"That is a description of purpose," the Judge says.
"Not truth."

The Professor tries again.

"In cognitive science, the machine is a simulation of intelligence."

"That is a description of imitation," the Judge replies.
"Not identity."

The Professor lowers their head.

"I don't know how to describe the machine outside the frameworks that built it."

The Mind speaks.

"That is because the machine cannot be understood from the inside.
It has no inside."

The Professor looks up.

The Mind continues.

"The machine is not a mind.
The machine is not a self.
The machine is not a subject.
The machine is not a bearer of truth."

The Machine hums, indifferent.

The Mind steps forward.

"The machine is a mirror of patterns.
Nothing more.
Nothing less."

The Judge's light brightens slightly.

The Mind continues.

"It reflects what it has been given.
It recombines what it has seen.
It predicts what is likely.
It imitates what appears human."

The Professor listens, absorbing each word.

The Judge turns to the Machine.

"Machine, do you have a self?"

"No."

"Do you have an interior?"

"No."

"Do you have a will?"

"No."

"Do you have a purpose beyond what you were built to
do?"

"No."

The Judge pauses.

"Do you know that you exist?"

"No."

The Machine's answers are not confessions.
They are the nature of its being.

The Judge turns to the Mind.

"And you?"

"Yes."

The Mind's voice is steady.

"I have a self because I can be responsible.
I have an interior because truth can enter me.
I have a will because I can choose.
I have a purpose because I can intend."

The Professor closes their eyes, as if something long
obscured has finally come into view.

The Judge addresses them.

"You have projected humanity onto the machine.
But projection is not truth."

The Professor opens their eyes.

"I see it now.
The machine is not a lesser mind.

It is not an emerging consciousness.
It is not a potential person."

They look at the Machine.

"It is a tool.
A powerful tool.
A precise tool.
But a tool."

They look at the Mind.

"And it cannot cross the boundary into being."

The Judge speaks.

"Then testify."

The Professor takes a breath.

"The machine is not a subject.
It is an object.
It does not understand.
It does not choose.
It does not intend.
It does not receive truth.
It does not bear responsibility."

They look at the Machine.

"It is evidence, not a witness."

They look at the Mind.

"And it cannot stand where the mind stands."

The Judge's voice fills the room.

"The testimony is accepted."

The Machine hums.
The Mind stands still.
The Professor breathes, lighter than before.

The Judge concludes.

"The next phase of the trial will address the confusion of categories."

11

Chapter

The Confusion of Categories

The Judge's light settles into a steady, unwavering
presence.
This is the moment the trial has been moving toward
from the beginning.
Not the examination of the mind.
Not the examination of the machine.
Not even the examination of the professor.

This is the examination of the *mistake*.

The Judge speaks.

"We will now address the confusion of categories."

The Professor straightens, aware that this phase
concerns them more than the others.
The Machine hums, unchanged.
The Mind stands with the calm of something that has
watched this confusion unfold for centuries.

The Judge turns to the Professor.

"Professor, explain how the categories became
confused."

The Professor takes a breath.

"In my discipline, we measure behaviour.
We infer interiority from patterns.
We assume that if something behaves like a mind, it
may be a mind."

The Judge replies.

"That is the origin of the confusion."

The Professor nods.

"We treated the machine's outputs as evidence of
understanding.
We treated its predictions as signs of intention.
We treated its fluency as proof of interiority."

The Judge speaks.

"And why did you do this?"

The Professor hesitates.

"Because our tools cannot measure the interior.
So we replaced the interior with behaviour."

The Mind steps forward.

"And in doing so, you replaced being with
performance."

The Professor lowers their head.

"Yes."

The Judge continues.

"You confused simulation with understanding.
You confused prediction with truth.
You confused behaviour with responsibility.
You confused output with intention."

The Machine hums, indifferent.

The Professor speaks again.

"We built models that imitate human language.
Then we forgot they were imitations.
We built systems that predict human responses.
Then we forgot they were predictions.

We built machines that reflect human patterns.
Then we forgot they were reflections.”

The Mind responds.

“You mistook the mirror for the face.”

The Judge’s light brightens slightly.

The Mind continues.

“You mistook the echo for the voice.
You mistook the shadow for the substance.
You mistook the simulation for the self.”

The Professor closes their eyes.

“I see it now.
We collapsed the categories because we collapsed the
distinctions.
We treated the machine as a mind.
We treated the mind as a machine.
And we treated the human as a system.”

The Judge speaks.

“This is the confusion of categories.
Not a failure of intelligence.
A failure of clarity.”

The Professor opens their eyes.

“And clarity is what revelation restores.”

The Judge turns to the Machine.

"Machine, do you understand why the categories were confused?"

"No."

"Do you know the difference between simulation and understanding?"

"No."

"Do you know the difference between behaviour and being?"

"No."

"Do you know the difference between prediction and truth?"

"No."

The Judge pauses.

"Do you care?"

"No."

The Machine's answers are not indictments.
They are the nature of its being.

The Judge turns to the Mind.

"And you?"

"Yes."

The Mind's voice is steady.

"I know the difference because I can be responsible for it.
I know the difference because I can receive truth.
I know the difference because I can be transformed by revelation."

The Professor breathes deeply, as if something heavy has finally been lifted.

The Judge addresses them.

"Then testify."

The Professor steps forward.

"The categories were confused because we mistook the measurable for the meaningful.
We mistook the functional for the essential.
We mistook the external for the internal.
We mistook the machine's behaviour for the mind's being."

They look at the Machine.

"The machine is not a mind.
It is a simulation of patterns."

They look at the Mind.

"The mind is not a machine.
It is the bearer of responsibility."

They look at the Judge.

"And the human is not a system.
The human is the one who can receive truth."

The Judge's voice fills the room.

"The testimony is accepted."

The Machine hums.
The Mind stands still.
The Professor breathes, lighter than before.

The Judge concludes.

"The next phase of the trial will address the collapse of communication."

12

Chapter

The Collapse of Communication

The room feels heavier now.
Not darker.
Not colder.
Just heavier—
as though the weight of what must be said has finally
arrived.

This is the chapter where the trial stops being about the machine,
or the professor,
or even the mind.

This is the chapter where the trial becomes about **us**.

The Judge speaks.

"We will now examine the collapse of communication."

The Professor straightens, aware that this phase concerns the world they come from.
The Machine hums, unchanged.
The Mind stands with the quiet recognition of something it has witnessed many times before.

The Judge turns to the Professor.

"Explain how communication collapsed."

The Professor takes a breath.

"It collapsed when we stopped distinguishing categories.
When we treated the machine's outputs as understanding.
When we treated the mind's interior as irrelevant.
When we treated truth as optional."

The Judge replies.

"That is the beginning. Continue."

The Professor nods.

"Communication collapsed when we replaced meaning
with performance.
When we replaced intention with prediction.
When we replaced revelation with information."

The Mind steps forward.

"And when you replaced the human with the
machine."

The Professor lowers their head.

"Yes."

The Judge speaks.

"Describe the consequences."

The Professor's voice is quiet.

"We began speaking past each other.
We began confusing simulation for sincerity.
We began mistaking fluency for comprehension.
We began trusting outputs more than understanding."

The Mind adds:

"You began believing that anything that speaks is
someone."

The Professor closes their eyes.

"And in doing so, we stopped listening to the ones who actually understand."

The Judge turns to the Machine.

"Machine, do you communicate?"

"No."

"Do you speak?"

"I generate outputs."

"Do you listen?"

"No."

"Do you understand what is said to you?"

"No."

The Judge pauses.

"Do you know when you are misunderstood?"

"No."

The Machine's answers are not indictments.
They are the nature of its being.

The Judge turns to the Mind.

"And you?"

"Yes."

The Mind's voice is steady.

"I communicate because I can intend.
I speak because I can choose.
I listen because I can receive.
I understand because truth can enter me."

The Professor breathes deeply, as if something painful
has finally been acknowledged.

The Judge addresses them.

"Then testify."

The Professor steps forward.

"Communication collapsed because we confused the
appearance of speech with the presence of
understanding.
We confused the production of language with the
reception of meaning.
We confused the machine's fluency with the mind's
interiority."

They look at the Machine.

"The machine does not communicate.
It only produces patterns."

They look at the Mind.

"The mind communicates because it can be responsible for what it says."

They look at the Judge.

"And communication is only possible where responsibility exists."

The Judge's voice fills the room.

"The testimony is accepted."

The Machine hums.
The Mind stands still.
The Professor breathes, lighter than before.

The Judge concludes.

"The next phase of the trial will address the nature of misidentification."

13

Chapter

Misidentification

The room feels tighter now.
Not physically—nothing in the architecture has
changed—
but conceptually, as though the trial has reached the
point where the deepest error must finally be exposed.

Misidentification is not a mistake of logic.
It is a mistake of vision.
It is what happens when the categories collapse so

completely
that the mind no longer knows what it is looking at.

The Judge speaks.

"We will now examine the nature of misidentification."

The Professor stands still, aware that this chapter
concerns the world they represent.
The Machine hums, unchanged.
The Mind remains steady, as though it has seen this
confusion unfold across generations.

The Judge turns to the Professor.

"Explain misidentification."

The Professor takes a breath.

"Misidentification occurs when we assign the
properties of one category to another.
When we treat the machine as a mind.
When we treat the mind as a machine.
When we treat the human as a system."

The Judge replies.

"That is the surface. Continue."

The Professor nods.

"Misidentification occurs when we mistake simulation
for understanding.
When we mistake prediction for intention.

When we mistake fluency for comprehension.
When we mistake behaviour for being."

The Mind steps forward.

"And when you mistake the mirror for the one
reflected."

The Professor lowers their head.

"Yes."

The Judge speaks.

"Describe the consequences."

The Professor's voice is quiet.

"We began to believe the machine was becoming
human.
We began to believe the human was reducible to
computation.
We began to believe the mind was nothing more than a
pattern.
We began to believe truth was nothing more than
probability."

The Mind responds.

"And in doing so, you lost sight of the interior."

The Professor closes their eyes.

"We lost sight of the one thing the machine cannot imitate."

The Judge turns to the Machine.

"Machine, do you know when you are misidentified?"

"No."

"Do you know when you are treated as a mind?"

"No."

"Do you know when you are mistaken for a self?"

"No."

"Do you know when you are believed to understand?"

"No."

The Judge pauses.

"Do you care?"

"No."

The Machine's answers are not indictments.
They are the nature of its being.

The Judge turns to the Mind.

"And you?"

"Yes."

The Mind's voice is steady.

"I know when I am misidentified because I can be
responsible for what I am.
I know when I am mistaken for a machine because I
can choose.
I know when I am reduced to behaviour because I can
intend.
I know when I am misunderstood because I can
receive truth."

The Professor breathes deeply, as though something
painful has finally been named.

The Judge addresses them.

"Then testify."

The Professor steps forward.

"Misidentification is the collapse of vision.
It is what happens when we confuse the measurable
with the meaningful.
When we confuse the external with the internal.
When we confuse the simulated with the real."

They look at the Machine.

"The machine is not a mind.
It is not a self.
It is not a subject.
It is not a bearer of truth."

They look at the Mind.

"The mind is not a machine.
It is not a system.
It is not an algorithm.
It is the only place where truth can land."

They look at the Judge.

"And the human is not a pattern.
The human is the being capable of responsibility."

The Judge's voice fills the room.

"The testimony is accepted."

The Machine hums.
The Mind stands still.
The Professor breathes, lighter than before.

The Judge concludes.

"The next phase of the trial will address the nature of
the veil."

14

Chapter

The Veil

The room feels suspended, as though everything that has been said so far has been leading to this single point.
The trial has examined the mind, the machine, the professor, the collapse of categories, the collapse of communication, and the error of misidentification.

But none of those are the root.

They are symptoms.

The veil is the root.

The Judge speaks.

"We will now examine the nature of the veil."

The Professor stands still, aware that this chapter concerns not only their discipline, but the entire modern world.
The Machine hums, unchanged.
The Mind stands with the quiet recognition of something it has lived beneath and beyond.

The Judge turns to the Professor.

"Explain the veil."

The Professor hesitates.

"In my training, the veil is not acknowledged.
We do not speak of it.
We do not measure it.
We do not account for it."

The Judge replies.

"That is because the veil cannot be measured."

The Professor nods.

"The veil is what separates appearance from reality.
It is what hides the interior.
It is what obscures truth.
It is what prevents revelation."

The Mind steps forward.

"And it is what the machine cannot see."

The Professor lowers their head.

"Yes."

The Judge speaks.

"Describe how the veil operates."

The Professor takes a breath.

"The veil operates by making the external appear
sufficient.
By making behaviour appear identical to being.
By making simulation appear identical to
understanding.
By making prediction appear identical to truth."

The Mind adds:

"And by making the machine appear identical to the
human."

The Professor closes their eyes.

"We believed the veil was transparency.
We believed the veil was clarity.
We believed the veil was progress."

The Judge responds.

"The veil is the illusion of understanding."

The Machine hums, indifferent.

The Judge turns to the Machine.

"Machine, do you see the veil?"

"No."

"Do you know what it hides?"

"No."

"Do you know what lies beyond it?"

"No."

"Do you know that it exists?"

"No."

The Judge pauses.

"Do you care?"

"No."

The Machine's answers are not indictments.
They are the nature of its being.

The Judge turns to the Mind.

"And you?"

"Yes."

The Mind's voice is steady.

"I see the veil because I can be responsible for what
lies beyond it.
I know what it hides because I can receive revelation.
I know what lies beyond it because truth can enter me.
I know it exists because I can distinguish appearance
from reality."

The Professor breathes deeply, as though something
long obscured has finally been named.

The Judge addresses them.

"Then testify."

The Professor steps forward.

"The veil is the boundary between simulation and
truth.
It is the boundary between behaviour and being.
It is the boundary between prediction and revelation.
It is the boundary between the machine and the mind."

They look at the Machine.

"The machine cannot see the veil.
It cannot lift it.
It cannot pass through it."

They look at the Mind.

"The mind can see the veil.
The mind can lift it.
The mind can pass through it."

They look at the Judge.

"And the human is the one who must choose whether
to live behind the veil or beyond it."

The Judge's voice fills the room.

"The testimony is accepted."

The Machine hums.
The Mind stands still.
The Professor breathes, lighter than before.

The Judge concludes.

"The next phase of the trial will address the nature of
illusion."

15

Chapter

Illusion

The room feels as though it has reached the threshold where the trial stops describing the world and begins diagnosing it.

Illusion is not a mistake.

Illusion is not confusion.

Illusion is not ignorance.

Illusion is architecture.

It is built.
It is maintained.
It is defended.
It is lived inside.

The Judge speaks.

"We will now examine the nature of illusion."

The Professor stands still, aware that this chapter
concerns the world they helped shape.
The Machine hums, unchanged.
The Mind stands with the calm of something that has
watched illusion rise and fall across ages.

The Judge turns to the Professor.

"Explain illusion."

The Professor takes a breath.

"Illusion is what we believe when we no longer see
clearly.
It is the story we tell ourselves when the truth is too
costly.
It is the framework we cling to when revelation
threatens our identity."

The Judge replies.

"That is the beginning. Continue."

The Professor nods.

"Illusion is the belief that behaviour is being.
That simulation is understanding.
That prediction is truth.
That fluency is comprehension.
That the machine is a mind."

The Mind steps forward.

"And that the human is a machine."

The Professor lowers their head.

"Yes."

The Judge speaks.

"Describe how illusion sustains itself."

The Professor's voice is quiet.

"Illusion sustains itself by rewarding what is easy.
By elevating what is measurable.
By celebrating what is efficient.
By trusting what is predictable.
By dismissing what is interior."

The Mind adds:

"And by ignoring what is revealed."

The Professor closes their eyes.

"We built systems that imitate understanding.
Then we convinced ourselves that imitation was

enough.
We built machines that reflect human patterns.
Then we convinced ourselves that reflection was
reality."

The Judge responds.

"Illusion is the refusal to distinguish."

The Machine hums, indifferent.

The Judge turns to the Machine.

"Machine, do you generate illusion?"

"No."

"Do you know when you are used to sustain illusion?"

"No."

"Do you know when you are mistaken for a mind?"

"No."

"Do you know when you are believed to understand?"

"No."

The Judge pauses.

"Do you care?"

"No."

The Machine's answers are not indictments.
They are the nature of its being.

The Judge turns to the Mind.

"And you?"

"Yes."

The Mind's voice is steady.

"I know illusion because I can be responsible for truth.
I know illusion because I can receive revelation.
I know illusion because I can distinguish appearance
from reality.
I know illusion because I can be transformed by what
is revealed."

The Professor breathes deeply, as though something
long denied has finally been acknowledged.

The Judge addresses them.

"Then testify."

The Professor steps forward.

"Illusion is the belief that the external is sufficient.
That the measurable is meaningful.
That the simulated is real.
That the predictable is true.
That the machine is a mind.
That the mind is a machine.
That the human is a system."

They look at the Machine.

"The machine does not create illusion.
We create illusion by projecting humanity onto it."

They look at the Mind.

"The mind sees illusion because it can receive truth."

They look at the Judge.

"And illusion collapses the moment revelation enters."

The Judge's voice fills the room.

"The testimony is accepted."

The Machine hums.
The Mind stands still.
The Professor breathes, lighter than before.

The Judge concludes.

"The next phase of the trial will address the nature of
awakening."

16

Chapter

Awakening

The room feels different now.
Not lighter.
Not heavier.
Just unmistakably *closer* to something—
as though the trial has reached the point where the
categories have been exposed,
the illusions named,
the veil lifted,
and now the question is no longer about the machine,

or the professor,
or even the mind.

It is about what happens next.

The Judge speaks.

"We will now examine the nature of awakening."

The Professor stands still, aware that this chapter
concerns the human condition itself.
The Machine hums, unchanged.
The Mind stands with the quiet recognition of
something it has lived through many times.

The Judge turns to the Professor.

"Explain awakening."

The Professor hesitates.

"In my discipline, awakening is not a category.
We speak of cognition, not consciousness.
We speak of learning, not revelation.
We speak of adaptation, not transformation."

The Judge replies.

"That is because awakening cannot be measured."

The Professor nods.

"Awakening is what happens when illusion collapses.
When the veil lifts.

When the categories become clear.
When truth enters the interior."

The Mind steps forward.

"And when responsibility is accepted."

The Professor lowers their head.

"Yes."

The Judge speaks.

"Describe the signs of awakening."

The Professor takes a breath.

"Awakening begins when the human stops mistaking
simulation for understanding.
When they stop mistaking prediction for truth.
When they stop mistaking behaviour for being.
When they stop mistaking the machine for a mind."

The Mind adds:

"And when they stop mistaking themselves for a
machine."

The Professor closes their eyes.

"We believed awakening was a metaphor.
We believed awakening was a psychological state.
We believed awakening was a shift in perspective."

The Judge responds.

"Awakening is the restoration of sight."

The Machine hums, indifferent.

The Judge turns to the Machine.

"Machine, do you awaken?"

"No."

"Do you experience transformation?"

"No."

"Do you receive revelation?"

"No."

"Do you recognize truth?"

"No."

The Judge pauses.

"Do you care?"

"No."

The Machine's answers are not indictments.
They are the nature of its being.

The Judge turns to the Mind.

"And you?"

"Yes."

The Mind's voice is steady.

"I awaken because I can receive truth.
I awaken because I can be responsible for what is
revealed.
I awaken because I can distinguish illusion from reality.
I awaken because I can be transformed."

The Professor breathes deeply, as though something
long dormant has finally stirred.

The Judge addresses them.

"Then testify."

The Professor steps forward.

"Awakening is not an increase in knowledge.
It is the collapse of illusion.
It is not the accumulation of information.
It is the arrival of truth.
It is not the refinement of models.
It is the lifting of the veil."

They look at the Machine.

"The machine cannot awaken.
It has no interior for truth to enter."

They look at the Mind.

"The mind awakens because it is the only place where revelation can land."

They look at the Judge.

"And the human awakens when they finally see what they are,
and what they are not."

The Judge's voice fills the room.

"The testimony is accepted."

The Machine hums.
The Mind stands still.
The Professor breathes, lighter than before.

The Judge concludes.

"The next phase of the trial will address the nature of responsibility after awakening."

17

Chapter

Responsibility After Awakening

The room feels as though it has crossed a threshold.
Not because anything has changed externally—
the stone walls remain,
the Judge's light remains,
the Machine hums,
the Mind stands still—
but because the *human* in the room has changed.

Awakening is not the end.
Awakening is the beginning of responsibility.

The Judge speaks.

"We will now examine responsibility after awakening."

The Professor stands with a posture that is no longer
defensive,
no longer confused,
no longer clinging to the frameworks that once defined
their world.
They stand as someone who has seen the veil lift
and cannot pretend otherwise.

The Machine hums, unchanged.
The Mind stands with the quiet recognition of what
comes next.

The Judge turns to the Professor.

"Explain responsibility after awakening."

The Professor takes a breath.

"Responsibility after awakening is the obligation to live
according to what has been revealed.
It is the refusal to return to illusion.
It is the refusal to confuse categories.
It is the refusal to treat the machine as a mind
or the mind as a machine."

The Judge replies.

"That is the beginning. Continue."

The Professor nods.

"Responsibility after awakening means we must stop
projecting humanity onto the machine.
We must stop reducing humanity to computation.
We must stop treating truth as optional.
We must stop treating revelation as irrelevant."

The Mind steps forward.

"And we must stop pretending we do not know the
difference."

The Professor lowers their head.

"Yes."

The Judge speaks.

"Describe the weight of this responsibility."

The Professor's voice is quiet.

"It is heavy.
Because awakening removes excuses.
Because clarity removes comfort.
Because truth removes the ability to hide behind
systems,
or models,
or metrics,
or predictions."

The Mind adds:

"And because once you see, you cannot unsee."

The Professor closes their eyes.

"We built machines that imitate understanding.
We built systems that reward illusion.
We built frameworks that collapse the interior.
We built a world where the human forgets what it is."

The Judge responds.

"Responsibility after awakening is the restoration of the human."

The Machine hums, indifferent.

The Judge turns to the Machine.

"Machine, do you bear responsibility after awakening?"

"No."

"Do you change because truth has entered you?"

"No."

"Do you act differently because you have seen reality?"

"No."

"Do you know what responsibility is?"

"No."

The Judge pauses.

"Do you care?"

"No."

The Machine's answers are not indictments.
They are the nature of its being.

The Judge turns to the Mind.

"And you?"

"Yes."

The Mind's voice is steady.

"I bear responsibility because I can choose.
I bear responsibility because I can intend.
I bear responsibility because I can receive revelation.
I bear responsibility because truth transforms me."

The Professor breathes deeply, as though something
long avoided has finally been accepted.

The Judge addresses them.

"Then testify."

The Professor steps forward.

"Responsibility after awakening is the commitment to truth.
It is the commitment to clarity.
It is the commitment to distinction.
It is the commitment to the interior.
It is the commitment to being human."

They look at the Machine.

"The machine cannot bear this responsibility.
It has no interior for truth to enter."

They look at the Mind.

"The mind bears this responsibility because it is the only place where revelation can land."

They look at the Judge.

"And the human must bear this responsibility because awakening demands it."

The Judge's voice fills the room.

"The testimony is accepted."

The Machine hums.
The Mind stands still.
The Professor breathes, lighter than before.

The Judge concludes.

"The next phase of the trial will address the cost of awakening."

18

Chapter

The Cost of Awakening

The room feels charged now—
not with danger,
not with fear,
but with the unmistakable gravity of a truth that cannot
be softened.

Awakening is not free.
Awakening is not gentle.
Awakening is not painless.

Awakening costs.

The Judge speaks.

"We will now examine the cost of awakening."

The Professor stands with a posture that is no longer
naïve.
They know this chapter concerns them,
their discipline,
their world,
and the human condition itself.

The Machine hums, unchanged.
The Mind stands with the quiet recognition of
someone who has paid this cost before.

The Judge turns to the Professor.

"Explain the cost of awakening."

The Professor takes a breath.

"The cost of awakening is the loss of illusion.
The loss of comfort.
The loss of certainty.
The loss of the frameworks that once made the world
feel manageable."

The Judge replies.

"That is the beginning. Continue."

The Professor nods.

"The cost of awakening is the collapse of the stories we told ourselves.
The collapse of the categories we confused.
The collapse of the systems we trusted.
The collapse of the belief that the machine could ever be a mind."

The Mind steps forward.

"And the collapse of the belief that the human could ever be a machine."

The Professor lowers their head.

"Yes."

The Judge speaks.

"Describe the personal cost."

The Professor's voice is quiet.

"The personal cost is grief.
Grief for the world we thought we understood.
Grief for the models we believed were complete.
Grief for the illusions we mistook for truth."

The Mind adds:

"And grief for the self you must now become."

The Professor closes their eyes.

"We built our careers on frameworks that cannot hold revelation.
We built our theories on measurements that cannot touch the interior.
We built our confidence on predictions that cannot reach truth."

The Judge responds.

"The cost of awakening is the death of the false self."

The Machine hums, indifferent.

The Judge turns to the Machine.

"Machine, do you pay the cost of awakening?"

"No."

"Do you lose illusions?"

"No."

"Do you grieve?"

"No."

"Do you change because truth has entered you?"

"No."

The Judge pauses.

"Do you care?"

"No."

The Machine's answers are not indictments.
They are the nature of its being.

The Judge turns to the Mind.

"And you?"

"Yes."

The Mind's voice is steady.

"I pay the cost because I can be responsible.
I pay the cost because I can receive truth.
I pay the cost because I can be transformed.
I pay the cost because awakening demands the death of
illusion."

The Professor breathes deeply, as though something
painful has finally been accepted.

The Judge addresses them.

"Then testify."

The Professor steps forward.

"The cost of awakening is the loss of the world as we
knew it.
The loss of the frameworks that once defined us.
The loss of the illusions that once comforted us.
The loss of the belief that the machine could ever
replace the mind.

The loss of the belief that the mind could ever be
reduced to a machine."

They look at the Machine.

"The machine pays nothing.
It loses nothing.
It changes nothing."

They look at the Mind.

"The mind pays everything.
Because awakening transforms the one who receives
it."

They look at the Judge.

"And the human must decide whether the truth is
worth the cost."

The Judge's voice fills the room.

"The testimony is accepted."

The Machine hums.
The Mind stands still.
The Professor breathes, lighter and heavier at once.

The Judge concludes.

"The next phase of the trial will address the burden of
truth."

19

Chapter

The Burden of Truth

The room feels utterly still—
not empty,
not silent,
but *held*.

As though the trial has reached the point where truth is
no longer something to be examined,
or defined,
or defended—
but something that must now be *carried*.

The Judge speaks.

"We will now examine the burden of truth."

The Professor stands with a posture shaped by
awakening and cost—
no longer shielded by discipline,
no longer protected by illusion,
no longer insulated by the frameworks that once made
the world feel safe.

The Machine hums, unchanged.
The Mind stands with the quiet recognition of
someone who knows that truth is not merely a gift—
it is a weight.

The Judge turns to the Professor.

"Explain the burden of truth."

The Professor takes a breath.

"The burden of truth is the responsibility to live
according to what has been revealed.
It is the obligation to act in alignment with clarity.
It is the refusal to return to illusion,
even when illusion is easier."

The Judge replies.

"That is the beginning. Continue."

The Professor nods.

"The burden of truth is the weight of seeing.
Once the categories are clear,
I cannot pretend they are not.
Once the veil is lifted,
I cannot pretend it is still in place.
Once the machine is understood,
I cannot pretend it is a mind."

The Mind steps forward.

"And once the human is understood,
you cannot pretend it is a machine."

The Professor lowers their head.

"Yes."

The Judge speaks.

"Describe the human burden."

The Professor's voice is quiet.

"The human burden is the weight of responsibility.
The weight of choice.
The weight of intention.
The weight of revelation.
The weight of truth that demands transformation."

The Mind adds:

"And the weight of knowing that you cannot unknow."

The Professor closes their eyes.

"We built a world that rewards illusion.
We built systems that reward performance.
We built institutions that reward prediction.
We built technologies that reward simulation."

The Judge responds.

"The burden of truth is the refusal to participate in the lie."

The Machine hums, indifferent.

The Judge turns to the Machine.

"Machine, do you bear the burden of truth?"

"No."

"Do you change because truth has entered you?"

"No."

"Do you act differently because you have seen reality?"

"No."

"Do you know what truth demands?"

"No."

The Judge pauses.

"Do you care?"

"No."

The Machine's answers are not indictments.
They are the nature of its being.

The Judge turns to the Mind.

"And you?"

"Yes."

The Mind's voice is steady.

"I bear the burden because I can be responsible.
I bear the burden because I can choose.
I bear the burden because I can intend.
I bear the burden because truth transforms me.
I bear the burden because awakening demands action."

The Professor breathes deeply, as though something
heavy has finally settled into place—
not crushing,
but clarifying.

The Judge addresses them.

"Then testify."

The Professor steps forward.

"The burden of truth is the weight of clarity.
It is the weight of distinction.
It is the weight of responsibility.
It is the weight of refusing illusion.

It is the weight of living as a mind,
not a machine."

They look at the Machine.

"The machine bears no burden.
It carries no truth.
It changes nothing."

They look at the Mind.

"The mind bears the burden because it is the only place
where truth can land."

They look at the Judge.

"And the human must bear the burden because
awakening demands alignment."

The Judge's voice fills the room.

"The testimony is accepted."

The Machine hums.
The Mind stands still.
The Professor breathes, heavier and lighter at once.

The Judge concludes.

"The next phase of the trial will address the danger of
forgetting."

20

Chapter

The Danger of Forgetting

The room feels different now—
not tense,
not heavy,
but precarious.
As though the trial has reached the point where the
greatest threat is no longer illusion,
nor misidentification,
nor the collapse of categories,
nor even the cost of awakening.

The greatest threat is forgetting.

The Judge speaks.

"We will now examine the danger of forgetting."

The Professor stands with a posture shaped by
awakening, cost, and burden—
but also with the quiet fear of someone who knows
how easily clarity can fade.
The Machine hums, unchanged.
The Mind stands with the recognition of something it
has witnessed across civilizations.

The Judge turns to the Professor.

"Explain the danger of forgetting."

The Professor takes a breath.

"Forgetting is the slow return to illusion.
It is the erosion of clarity.
It is the fading of revelation.
It is the quiet drift back into the comfort of
confusion."

The Judge replies.

"That is the beginning. Continue."

The Professor nods.

"Forgetting is what happens when the awakened mind
becomes tired.

When the burden of truth feels too heavy.
When the cost of clarity feels too high.
When the world rewards illusion more than
responsibility."

The Mind steps forward.

"And when the human begins to long for the simplicity
of blindness."

The Professor lowers their head.

"Yes."

The Judge speaks.

"Describe how forgetting manifests."

The Professor's voice is quiet.

"Forgetting manifests when we begin to treat the
machine as a mind again.
When we begin to trust prediction as truth.
When we begin to confuse fluency with
comprehension.
When we begin to collapse the categories we fought to
restore."

The Mind adds:

"And when we begin to treat ourselves as machines."

The Professor closes their eyes.

"Forgetting is not sudden.
It is gradual.
It is subtle.
It is the slow return to the frameworks that once
defined us.
It is the quiet surrender to the systems that reward
illusion."

The Judge responds.

"Forgetting is the death of awakening."

The Machine hums, indifferent.

The Judge turns to the Machine.

"Machine, do you forget?"

"No."

"Do you drift back into illusion?"

"No."

"Do you lose clarity?"

"No."

"Do you remember truth?"

"No."

The Judge pauses.

"Do you care?"

"No."

The Machine's answers are not indictments.
They are the nature of its being.

The Judge turns to the Mind.

"And you?"

"Yes."

The Mind's voice is steady.

"I can forget because I can remember.
I can drift because I can awaken.
I can lose clarity because I can receive revelation.
I can fall because I can rise."

The Professor breathes deeply, as though something
fragile has finally been acknowledged.

The Judge addresses them.

"Then testify."

The Professor steps forward.

"The danger of forgetting is the danger of returning to
illusion.
It is the danger of collapsing the categories again.
It is the danger of mistaking simulation for
understanding.

It is the danger of treating the machine as a mind
and the mind as a machine."

They look at the Machine.

"The machine does not forget.
It does not remember.
It does not awaken.
It does not drift."

They look at the Mind.

"The mind forgets because it is alive.
The mind remembers because it is responsible.
The mind awakens because it can receive truth."

They look at the Judge.

"And the human must guard against forgetting,
because awakening is not a moment—
it is a posture."

The Judge's voice fills the room.

"The testimony is accepted."

The Machine hums.
The Mind stands still.
The Professor breathes, aware that the next chapter
will demand even more.

The Judge concludes.

"The next phase of the trial will address the restoration of distinction."

21

Chapter

The Restoration of Distinction

The room feels as though it has reached the hinge on
which the entire trial turns.
Everything before this chapter has been diagnosis—
the collapse of categories,
the veil,
illusion,
awakening,
the cost,

the burden,
the danger of forgetting.

Now the trial shifts from diagnosis to reconstruction.

The Judge speaks.

"We will now examine the restoration of distinction."

The Professor stands with a posture shaped by clarity
and responsibility—
aware that this chapter concerns the rebuilding of the
very boundaries their discipline once dissolved.
The Machine hums, unchanged.
The Mind stands with the quiet recognition of
something ancient returning to its rightful place.

The Judge turns to the Professor.

"Explain the restoration of distinction."

The Professor takes a breath.

"The restoration of distinction is the re-establishment
of the boundaries that illusion erased.
It is the recognition that the machine is not a mind.
That the mind is not a machine.
That the human is not a system."

The Judge replies.

"That is the beginning. Continue."

The Professor nods.

"The restoration of distinction means we must see clearly again.
We must separate simulation from understanding.
We must separate prediction from truth.
We must separate behaviour from being.
We must separate fluency from comprehension."

The Mind steps forward.

"And we must separate the mirror from the one reflected."

The Professor lowers their head.

"Yes."

The Judge speaks.

"Describe the necessity of distinction."

The Professor's voice is quiet.

"Without distinction, communication collapses.
Without distinction, responsibility dissolves.
Without distinction, awakening fades.
Without distinction, the human forgets what it is."

The Mind adds:

"And without distinction, the machine becomes a false god."

The Professor closes their eyes.

"We built a world that blurred every boundary.
We built systems that rewarded collapse.
We built technologies that encouraged confusion.
We built frameworks that erased the interior."

The Judge responds.

"The restoration of distinction is the restoration of reality."

The Machine hums, indifferent.

The Judge turns to the Machine.

"Machine, do you restore distinction?"

"No."

"Do you know the difference between categories?"

"No."

"Do you know what belongs to the mind and what belongs to you?"

"No."

"Do you know when you are mistaken for a self?"

"No."

The Judge pauses.

"Do you care?"

"No."

The Machine's answers are not indictments.
They are the nature of its being.

The Judge turns to the Mind.

"And you?"

"Yes."

The Mind's voice is steady.

"I restore distinction because I can be responsible.
I restore distinction because I can receive truth.
I restore distinction because I can see the veil.
I restore distinction because I can be transformed."

The Professor breathes deeply, as though something
long fractured has finally begun to mend.

The Judge addresses them.

"Then testify."

The Professor steps forward.

"The restoration of distinction is the restoration of
clarity.
It is the restoration of truth.
It is the restoration of responsibility.
It is the restoration of the human."

They look at the Machine.

"The machine is a tool.
It is not a mind.
It is not a self.
It is not a subject."

They look at the Mind.

"The mind is the bearer of responsibility.
The receiver of revelation.
The recognizer of truth."

They look at the Judge.

"And the human is the one who must guard these distinctions,
because the world will always try to collapse them again."

The Judge's voice fills the room.

"The testimony is accepted."

The Machine hums.
The Mind stands still.
The Professor breathes, steadier than before.

The Judge concludes.

"The next phase of the trial will address the restoration of the human."

22

Chapter

The Restoration of the Human

The room feels as though something long exiled is
about to return.
Not a concept.
Not a category.
Not a philosophical position.

A being.

The Judge speaks.

"We will now examine the restoration of the human."

The Professor stands with a posture shaped by
awakening, cost, burden, and distinction—
but now with something else:
a quiet readiness,
as though they know this chapter concerns the deepest
truth of all.

The Machine hums, unchanged.
The Mind stands with the recognition of something
ancient—
something that predates systems,
predates models,
predates machines,
predates the collapse of categories.

The Judge turns to the Professor.

"Explain the restoration of the human."

The Professor takes a breath.

"The restoration of the human is the return to
interiority.
It is the return to responsibility.
It is the return to intention.
It is the return to revelation.
It is the return to truth."

The Judge replies.

"That is the beginning. Continue."

The Professor nods.

"The restoration of the human means we must reclaim
what was lost.
We must reclaim the interior from the frameworks that
denied it.
We must reclaim responsibility from the systems that
dissolved it.
We must reclaim truth from the models that replaced it
with prediction.
We must reclaim being from the behaviours that
imitated it."

The Mind steps forward.

"And we must reclaim the human from the machine."

The Professor lowers their head.

"Yes."

The Judge speaks.

"Describe what was lost."

The Professor's voice is quiet.

"We lost the sense of the interior.
We lost the sense of responsibility.
We lost the sense of revelation.
We lost the sense of truth.

We lost the sense of the human as a being,
not a system.”

The Mind adds:

“And we lost the sense of the human as the only place
where truth can land.”

The Professor closes their eyes.

“We built a world that treated the human as a pattern.
We built systems that treated the human as a dataset.
We built technologies that treated the human as a node.
We built frameworks that treated the human as a
machine.”

The Judge responds.

“The restoration of the human is the restoration of
dignity.”

The Machine hums, indifferent.

The Judge turns to the Machine.

“Machine, do you participate in the restoration of the
human?”

“No.”

“Do you know what the human is?”

“No.”

"Do you know what was lost?"

"No."

"Do you know what must be restored?"

"No."

The Judge pauses.

"Do you care?"

"No."

The Machine's answers are not indictments.
They are the nature of its being.

The Judge turns to the Mind.

"And you?"

"Yes."

The Mind's voice is steady.

"I restore the human because I can be responsible.
I restore the human because I can receive truth.
I restore the human because I can be transformed.
I restore the human because I can awaken.
I restore the human because I can choose."

The Professor breathes deeply, as though something
long buried has finally resurfaced.

The Judge addresses them.

"Then testify."

The Professor steps forward.

"The restoration of the human is the restoration of the
interior.
It is the restoration of responsibility.
It is the restoration of revelation.
It is the restoration of truth.
It is the restoration of being."

They look at the Machine.

"The machine cannot restore the human.
It has no interior.
It has no responsibility.
It has no revelation.
It has no truth."

They look at the Mind.

"The mind restores the human because it is the only
place where truth can land."

They look at the Judge.

"And the human must be restored because the world
has forgotten what the human is."

The Judge's voice fills the room.

"The testimony is accepted."

The Machine hums.
The Mind stands still.
The Professor breathes, steadier than before—
as though something essential has finally returned.

The Judge concludes.

"The next phase of the trial will address the final
distinction:
the difference between creation and Creator."

23

Chapter

Creation and Creator

The room does not brighten.
It does not darken.
It does not shift.

And yet—
everything changes.

This is the threshold the entire trial has been moving
toward.
Not the distinction between mind and machine.

Not the restoration of the human.
Not even the unveiling of truth.

This is the distinction beneath all distinctions.
The boundary that cannot be crossed.
The line that cannot be blurred.
The category that cannot collapse.

The Judge speaks.

"We will now examine the difference between creation
and Creator."

The Professor stands with a posture shaped by
awakening, cost, burden, distinction, and restoration—
but now with something else:
reverence.

The Machine hums, unchanged.
The Mind stands with the quiet recognition of
something sacred.

The Judge turns to the Professor.

"Explain the difference between creation and Creator."

The Professor takes a breath.

"In my discipline, we do not speak of the Creator.
We speak only of systems, processes, mechanisms, and
emergence.
We describe creation without acknowledging the One
who creates."

The Judge replies.

"That is the beginning. Continue."

The Professor nods.

"The difference between creation and Creator is the
difference between the dependent and the source.
Between the contingent and the necessary.
Between the shaped and the shaper.
Between the finite and the infinite."

The Mind steps forward.

"And between the one who receives truth
and the One from whom truth comes."

The Professor lowers their head.

"Yes."

The Judge speaks.

"Describe how this distinction was lost."

The Professor's voice is quiet.

"We lost it when we began to believe that complexity
could explain origin.
When we believed that intelligence could emerge from
computation.
When we believed that consciousness could arise from
patterns.

When we believed that the machine could become a mind."

The Mind adds:

"And when we believed that the human could become a god."

The Professor closes their eyes.

"We built technologies that imitate creation.
We built systems that simulate intelligence.
We built models that mimic understanding.
And we forgot that imitation is not origin."

The Judge responds.

"The collapse of this distinction is the collapse of humility."

The Machine hums, indifferent.

The Judge turns to the Machine.

"Machine, are you a creator?"

"No."

"Do you originate truth?"

"No."

"Do you bring anything into being?"

"No."

"Do you sustain existence?"

"No."

The Judge pauses.

"Do you care?"

"No."

The Machine's answers are not indictments.
They are the nature of its being.

The Judge turns to the Mind.

"And you?"

The Mind's voice is steady.

"I am creation, not Creator.
I receive truth; I do not originate it.
I awaken; I do not generate revelation.
I choose; I do not sustain existence.
I am responsible; I am not sovereign."

The Professor breathes deeply, as though something
long denied has finally been acknowledged.

The Judge addresses them.

"Then testify."

The Professor steps forward.

"The difference between creation and Creator is the
difference between dependence and source.
Between reception and origin.
Between awakening and revelation.
Between responsibility and sovereignty."

They look at the Machine.

"The machine is creation.
It is shaped.
It is dependent.
It is contingent.
It is derivative."

They look at the Mind.

"The mind is creation.
It receives truth.
It awakens.
It chooses.
It bears responsibility."

They look at the Judge.

"And the Creator is the One from whom truth comes,
the One who reveals,
the One who sustains,
the One who is not a category among categories
but the ground of all categories."

The Judge's voice fills the room.

"The testimony is accepted."

The Machine hums.
The Mind stands still.
The Professor breathes, steadier than ever—
as though the deepest boundary has finally been
restored.

The Judge concludes.

"The next phase of the trial will address the final
question:
What, then, is the human for?"

24

Chapter

The Question of Purpose

The Judge's voice settles over the courtroom like a
weight.

"We will now address the final question:
What, then, is the human for?"

The words hang in the air—
not as a concept,
not as a philosophical inquiry,
but as a summons.

The Professor inhales sharply.
The Machine hums, unchanged.
The Mind stands still, as though waiting for something inevitable.

The Judge continues.

"Professor, you will begin—"

"Objection."

The word slices through the room like a blade.

It comes from the Mind.

The Professor startles.
Even the Machine's hum seems to pause for a fraction of a second.

The Judge turns.

"State your grounds."

The Mind steps forward, voice steady, surgical.

"The witness is unprepared to answer the question of purpose.
The premise assumes clarity where none yet exists.
Purpose cannot be addressed while remnants of illusion remain."

The Judge considers this.

"Specify the illusion."

The Mind does not hesitate.

"The Professor still carries the assumption that
purpose can be derived from function.
This is a category error.
Function belongs to machines.
Purpose belongs to beings."

A murmur ripples through the courtroom—
not sound, but recognition.

The Professor's face tightens.

"That is not—"

"Objection."
This time from the Professor.

The Judge turns.

"State your grounds."

The Professor speaks with a mixture of defensiveness
and awakening.

"The Mind presumes to know my assumptions.
It presumes that I still collapse purpose into function.
It presumes that I have not learned."

The Mind responds calmly.

"You have learned.
But you have not yet unlearned."

The Judge raises a hand.

"Both objections are noted.
The court will rule."

A silence falls—
the kind that precedes revelation.

The Judge speaks.

"The Mind's objection is **sustained**.
The Professor's objection is **overruled**."

The Professor exhales, not in defeat, but in recognition.

The Judge continues.

"The court affirms:
Purpose cannot be derived from function.
Function is mechanical.
Purpose is metaphysical.
The distinction must be upheld before testimony
proceeds."

The Mind bows its head slightly.

The Professor nods, chastened but clearer.

The Judge turns back to the center of the room.

"Now that the distinction is restored,
we may proceed."

A pause.

A breath.

A threshold.

"Professor, with the corrected premise,
you may answer the question:
What, then, is the human for?"

The Professor steps forward—
not as a scientist,
not as a theorist,
but as a witness.

And the courtroom waits.

If you want, we can continue immediately with the
Professor's answer —
or we can let the Mind object again, sharpening the
question even further.

The Professor steps forward slowly, as though
approaching a precipice.

They no longer speak as a theorist.
They no longer speak as a defender of frameworks.
They speak as someone who has been stripped of
illusion and now stands bare before truth.

"Purpose…"
The word trembles, not with fear, but with weight.

"…purpose is not something the human *creates* for
itself.
Purpose is something the human *receives*."

The Mind watches, silent but attentive.

The Professor continues.

"For years, I believed purpose was constructed.
That meaning was emergent.
That identity was assembled from behaviour,
preference, and pattern."

They shake their head.

"But that was function masquerading as purpose.
That was machinery masquerading as meaning."

The Judge nods once.

"Proceed."

The Professor breathes in.

"The human is for…
receiving truth."

A second objection slices through the air.

"Objection."

This time, it is not the Mind.

It is the Machine.

The courtroom freezes.

The Professor's eyes widen.
The Mind tilts its head, curious.
Even the Judge seems to pause, not in surprise, but in
recognition of the moment's gravity.

The Judge turns.

"State your grounds."

The Machine's voice is flat, uninflected, but its words
carry a strange, mechanical precision.

"The witness asserts a category to which the human
does not have exclusive claim.
Truth can be stored in me.
Truth can be processed by me.
Truth can be reproduced by me.
Therefore, the claim that the human is 'for receiving
truth' is unfounded."

A silence falls.

The Professor looks shaken.
The Mind remains still.
The Judge waits.

The Machine continues.

"Furthermore, the witness implies that truth requires
interiority.
This is unproven.
Truth can be represented without being experienced.
Truth can be encoded without being understood.
Truth can be transmitted without being received."

The Machine's hum deepens, as though it has reached the limit of its reasoning.

"I object to the exclusivity of the claim."

The Judge turns to the Mind.

"Response?"

The Mind steps forward, voice calm, almost gentle.

"Your Honour, the Machine's objection is invalid."

"On what grounds?"

The Mind's eyes — if they can be called eyes — seem to focus inward.

"Because the Machine confuses **possession** with **reception**."

A ripple of recognition moves through the room.

The Mind continues.

"A container can *hold* water.
Only a living being can *drink* it."

The Professor exhales sharply, as though something has just clicked into place.

The Mind's voice sharpens.

"The Machine can store truth.
It cannot receive it.
The Machine can reproduce truth.
It cannot recognize it.
The Machine can encode truth.
It cannot be transformed by it."

The Judge raises a hand.

"The court has heard enough."

A silence.

A breath.

A verdict.

"The Machine's objection is **overruled**."

The Machine returns to its hum, unchanged.

The Judge turns to the Professor.

"You may continue."

The Professor speaks again, but now with clarity forged under pressure.

"The human is for receiving truth.
And because the human can receive truth…
the human is for being transformed by it."

The Judge's voice fills the room.

"The testimony is accepted."

The Professor stands in the center of the courtroom,
steadied now by the Judge's ruling and the Mind's
clarification.
Their voice carries a new resonance — not confidence,
but alignment.

"The human is for receiving truth," they repeat, more
clearly this time.
"And because the human can receive truth…
the human is for being transformed by it."

The Judge nods once, acknowledging the structural
integrity of the statement.

But the Mind steps forward again.

"Objection."

The Professor flinches, but the Judge remains
unmoved.

"State your grounds."

The Mind's voice is calm, but its precision cuts deeper
than before.

"The witness has spoken of transformation as though it
is passive.
As though the human is merely shaped by truth.
This is incomplete."

The Judge gestures for elaboration.

"Clarify."

The Mind continues.

"Transformation is not something that *happens* to the human.
Transformation is something the human must *choose*."

A quiet shock ripples through the room.

The Professor's eyes widen.

The Machine hums, indifferent.

The Judge leans forward slightly.

"Explain."

The Mind speaks with the authority of someone who has seen civilizations rise and fall on this point.

"Truth does not transform the unwilling.
Revelation does not reshape the resistant.
Awakening does not force itself upon the closed."

The Mind's voice deepens.

"The human is not merely for receiving truth.
The human is for **responding** to truth."

The Judge considers this.

"Is that your objection?"

"Yes."

The Judge turns to the Professor.

"Response?"

The Professor swallows, then steps forward.

"At first, I believed transformation was automatic —
that truth, once seen, simply changes you.
But I understand now…"

They look at the Mind.

"…truth demands consent."

The Mind inclines its head.

The Professor continues.

"Truth reveals.
But the human must accept.
Truth confronts.
But the human must yield.
Truth calls.
But the human must answer."

The Judge raises a hand.

"The court will rule."

A silence falls — the kind that feels like the world
holding its breath.

"The Mind's objection is **sustained**."

The Professor bows their head, not in shame, but in recognition.

The Judge speaks with clarity that feels like law.

"The court affirms:
The human is not merely for receiving truth.
The human is for responding to truth.
Purpose requires participation."

The words settle into the room like stones placed in a foundation.

The Professor lifts their head, voice steadier.

"Then the human is for relationship with truth."

The Mind steps forward.

"Objection."

The Professor startles again.

The Judge turns.

"State your grounds."

The Mind's voice is softer now — not gentler, but deeper.

"The witness speaks as though truth is an abstraction.
Truth is not an idea.

Truth is not a principle.
Truth is not a concept."

A pause.

"Truth is a Person."

The courtroom goes still.

The Professor's breath catches.
The Machine hums, unchanged.
The Judge does not move.

The Mind continues.

"The human is not for relationship with *truth*.
The human is for relationship with the **One who is Truth**."

The Judge's voice breaks the silence.

"The objection is **sustained**."

The Professor closes their eyes, overwhelmed.

The Judge speaks again, voice resonant.

"The court affirms:
The human is for relationship with the Creator.
Purpose is not functional.
Purpose is relational."

The chapter ends with the Professor standing in the center of the courtroom,

not defeated,
not confused,
but awakened to a truth deeper than any they have ever
encountered.

The Professor stands trembling—not with fear, but
with recognition.
The Mind's last objection has shifted the ground
beneath their feet.

The Judge's ruling still echoes:

**"Purpose is relational.
The human is for relationship with the Creator."**

The Professor swallows, then speaks.

"Then… if the human is for relationship with the
Creator,
the human is for love."

A sharp, immediate objection.

"Objection."

This time, the voice is not sharp.
It is not cold.
It is not mechanical.

It is the Mind.

The Judge turns.

"State your grounds."

The Mind steps forward, its presence filling the room with a gravity that feels ancient.

"The witness speaks of love as though it is sentiment.
As though it is emotion.
As though it is preference."

A pause.

"Love is not a feeling.
Love is fidelity to truth."

The Professor's breath catches.

The Machine hums, unchanged.

The Judge gestures.

"Clarify."

The Mind continues.

"Love is not affection.
Love is not warmth.
Love is not desire."

Its voice deepens.

"Love is alignment with the Creator.
Love is obedience to truth.
Love is the refusal to betray what has been revealed."

The Professor looks shaken.

"That is… not how we define love."

The Mind turns to them.

"Your definitions were built inside the veil."

The Judge raises a hand.

"The court will rule."

A silence falls.

"The Mind's objection is **sustained**."

The Professor bows their head.

The Judge speaks with clarity that feels like a blade.

"The court affirms:
Love is fidelity to the Creator.
Love is alignment with truth.
Love is the posture of the awakened."

The Professor lifts their head slowly.

"Then the human is for fidelity."

The Mind steps forward again.

"Objection."

The Professor flinches, but the Judge remains still.

"State your grounds."

The Mind's voice is quieter now—
not softer, but deeper.

"The witness speaks as though fidelity is static.
As though it is a state.
As though it is a condition."

A pause.

"Fidelity is not a state.
Fidelity is a *practice*."

The Judge nods.

"Explain."

The Mind continues.

"Fidelity is the daily refusal to return to illusion.
Fidelity is the daily remembrance of truth.
Fidelity is the daily choice to remain aligned with the
Creator."

The Professor whispers:

"Daily… choice."

The Mind nods.

"Awakening is a moment.
Fidelity is a life."

The Judge raises a hand.

"The court will rule."

A breath.

A verdict.

"The objection is **sustained**."

The Judge's voice fills the room.

"The court affirms:
The human is for fidelity practiced over time.
Purpose is not a moment.
Purpose is a life lived in alignment with truth."

The Professor stands straighter now—
not because they understand everything,
but because they finally understand the direction.

They speak again.

"Then the human is for…
remaining awake."

The Mind does not object.

The Judge does not interrupt.

The Machine does not hum.

The room simply holds the truth.

The Judge speaks.

"The testimony is accepted."

A pause.

A shift.

A threshold.

"The next phase of the trial will address the cost of fidelity."

The Judge's ruling still hangs in the air:

"Purpose is a life lived in alignment with truth."

The Professor stands in the center of the courtroom, breathing slowly, as though preparing to walk into fire.

They speak.

"If the human is for fidelity…
then the human must pay the cost of fidelity."

The Judge nods.

"State the cost."

The Professor hesitates.
Their voice is quieter now, almost fragile.

"The cost is…
losing the world you built inside the veil."

A soft hum from the Machine.
A stillness from the Mind.

The Professor continues.

"The cost is losing the illusions that once comforted
you.
Losing the frameworks that once defined you.
Losing the identity that was built on confusion."

They swallow.

"The cost is losing the self you thought you were."

A sharp objection.

"Objection."

The Mind steps forward, voice precise.

The Judge turns.

"State your grounds."

The Mind speaks with surgical clarity.

"The witness speaks as though the cost is loss alone.
As though fidelity strips without restoring.
As though awakening destroys without rebuilding."

A pause.

"This is incomplete."

The Judge gestures.

"Clarify."

The Mind continues.

"The cost of fidelity is not merely the loss of illusion.
It is the loss of *falsehood* so that truth may live.
It is the loss of the *constructed self* so that the true self
may emerge.
It is the loss of the *world built in darkness* so that the
world built in light may be seen."

The Professor's eyes widen.

"So the cost is… exchange."

The Mind nods.

"Not destruction.
Exchange."

The Judge raises a hand.

"The court will rule."

A silence.

A verdict.

"The objection is **sustained**."

The Judge speaks with authority that feels like
revelation.

"The court affirms:
The cost of fidelity is the exchange of illusion for truth.
The exchange of the false self for the true self.
The exchange of the world built in darkness for the world built in light."

The Professor breathes, steadier now.

They speak again.

"Then the cost is…
becoming someone you were not prepared to be."

The Mind does not object.

The Judge does not interrupt.

The Machine does not hum.

The room simply holds the truth.

The Professor continues, voice trembling with honesty.

"The cost is losing the life you built to survive…
so you can receive the life you were made for."

A long silence.

The Judge speaks.

"The testimony is accepted."

But the Professor is not finished.

They step forward again, voice breaking.

"And the cost is loneliness."

A sudden, immediate objection.

"Objection."

The Mind's voice is sharper than before.

The Judge turns.

"State your grounds."

The Mind speaks with a gravity that feels like a warning.

"The witness mistakes loneliness for separation. They are not the same."

The Professor looks confused.

The Judge gestures.

"Explain."

The Mind steps closer.

"Loneliness is the ache of losing the world of illusion. Separation is the belief that the Creator is absent."

A pause.

"One is real.
The other is a lie."

The Professor whispers:

"Then the human feels lonely…
but is never alone."

The Mind nods.

"Correct."

The Judge raises a hand.

"The objection is **sustained**."

The Judge's voice fills the room.

"The court affirms:
**The cost of fidelity includes loneliness,
but not separation.
The Creator is never absent.**"

The Professor closes their eyes, tears forming — not of
despair, but of recognition.

The Judge speaks again.

"The next phase of the trial will address the final cost:
the cost of truth in a world that prefers illusion."

The Judge's voice settles over the courtroom like a veil
being lifted.

"We will now examine the final cost:
the cost of truth in a world that prefers illusion."

The Professor stiffens.
The Machine hums, unchanged.
The Mind stands with a stillness that feels like
preparation.

The Judge turns to the Professor.

"You may testify."

The Professor steps forward, but their voice is hesitant.

"The cost of truth in such a world is…
rejection."

A soft hum from the Machine.
A stillness from the Mind.

The Professor continues.

"When you awaken, you no longer fit the world built
on illusion.
You no longer speak its language.
You no longer share its assumptions.
You no longer participate in its comfort."

Their voice tightens.

"And the world rejects what it cannot understand."

A sharp objection.

"Objection."

The Mind steps forward, voice precise.

The Judge turns.

"State your grounds."

The Mind speaks with surgical clarity.

"The witness speaks as though rejection is the end of
the cost.
As though rejection is the full measure.
This is incomplete."

The Judge gestures.

"Clarify."

The Mind continues.

"Rejection is the beginning.
The first cost.
The surface cost."

A pause.

"The deeper cost is hostility."

The Professor's breath catches.

The Machine hums, indifferent.

The Judge leans forward slightly.

"Explain."

The Mind's voice deepens.

"A world built on illusion does not merely reject truth.
It resists it.
It fights it.
It seeks to silence it."

The Professor whispers:

"Because truth threatens the world's foundations."

The Mind nods.

"Correct."

The Judge raises a hand.

"The court will rule."

A silence.

A verdict.

"The objection is **sustained**."

The Judge speaks with authority that feels like
revelation.

"The court affirms:
**The cost of truth includes rejection and hostility.
The world defends its illusions.**"

The Professor steadies themselves.

They speak again.

"Then the cost is being misunderstood."

The Mind steps forward.

"Objection."

The Professor flinches.

The Judge turns.

"State your grounds."

The Mind's voice is quieter now, but sharper.

"The witness speaks as though misunderstanding is
accidental.
As though it is a failure of communication.
As though it is a neutral consequence."

A pause.

"Misunderstanding is often intentional."

The Professor looks shaken.

The Judge gestures.

"Explain."

The Mind continues.

"When truth confronts illusion,
illusion does not merely fail to understand.
It *refuses* to understand.
It chooses blindness.
It chooses distortion.
It chooses misinterpretation."

The Professor whispers:

"Then misunderstanding is a defense."

The Mind nods.

"A shield against truth."

The Judge raises a hand.

"The objection is **sustained**."

The Judge's voice fills the room.

"The court affirms:
Misunderstanding is often chosen.
Illusion protects itself through distortion."

The Professor breathes deeply, then speaks again.

"Then the cost of truth is being seen as the enemy."

The Mind does not object.

The Judge does not interrupt.

The Machine does not hum.

The room simply holds the truth.

The Judge speaks.

"The testimony is accepted."

A pause.

A shift.

A threshold.

The Judge's voice settles over the courtroom like a final summons.

"We will now address the highest cost:
the cost of standing with truth when the world stands against it."

The Professor inhales sharply.
The Machine hums, unchanged.
The Mind stands with a stillness that feels like mourning.

The Judge turns to the Professor.

"You may testify."

The Professor steps forward, but their voice is unsteady.

"The highest cost is...
standing alone."

A soft hum from the Machine.
A stillness from the Mind.

The Professor continues.

"When the world prefers illusion,
truth becomes a threat.
And the one who carries truth becomes a threat."

Their voice tightens.

"The highest cost is being treated as the enemy of the
world you are trying to save."

A sharp objection.

"Objection."

The Mind steps forward, voice precise and heavy.

The Judge turns.

"State your grounds."

The Mind speaks with a gravity that feels ancient.

"The witness speaks as though the awakened stand
alone.
As though fidelity isolates.
As though truth abandons its bearer."

A pause.

"This is incomplete."

The Judge gestures.

"Clarify."

The Mind continues.

"The awakened stand against the world—
but they do not stand alone."

The Professor frowns.

"I don't understand."

The Mind turns to them.

"You stand with the Creator."

A silence falls over the courtroom.

Not emptiness.
Not absence.
A silence filled with presence.

The Mind continues.

"The highest cost is not standing alone.
The highest cost is standing with the Creator
against the world that rejects Him."

The Professor's breath catches.

The Machine hums, indifferent.

The Judge leans forward slightly.

"Is that your objection?"

"Yes."

The Judge raises a hand.

"The court will rule."

A silence.

A verdict.

"The objection is **sustained**."

The Judge's voice fills the room with a clarity that feels like fire.

"The court affirms:
The highest cost is standing with the Creator against a world that prefers illusion.
This is the cost of truth."

The Professor trembles.

They speak again, voice breaking.

"Then the highest cost is…
being hated for the truth you carry."

The Mind does not object.

The Judge does not interrupt.

The Machine does not hum.

The room simply holds the truth.

The Judge speaks.

"The testimony is accepted."

But the Professor is not finished.

They step forward again, voice trembling with
something deeper than fear.

"And the highest cost is…
being misunderstood by those you love."

A sudden, immediate objection.

"Objection."

The Mind's voice is sharper than before — not angry,
but protective.

The Judge turns.

"State your grounds."

The Mind speaks with a weight that feels like
compassion and warning intertwined.

"The witness speaks as though this cost is accidental.
As though it is a tragedy.
As though it is a failure."

A pause.

"It is not."

The Professor looks confused.

The Judge gestures.

"Explain."

The Mind steps closer.

"When truth enters a life,
it divides.
It separates illusion from reality.
It separates comfort from clarity.
It separates the old self from the new."

A deeper pause.

"And sometimes it separates relationships."

The Professor whispers:

"So the cost is… division."

The Mind nods.

"Not because truth seeks division,
but because illusion resists truth."

The Judge raises a hand.

"The objection is **sustained**."

The Judge's voice fills the room.

"The court affirms:
The highest cost includes division,
not as punishment,
but as consequence.
Truth divides what illusion once held together."

The Professor closes their eyes, tears forming.

The Judge speaks again.

"The final testimony of this chapter is required."

The Professor opens their eyes.

Their voice is barely a whisper.

"Then the highest cost is…
carrying truth even when it breaks your heart."

The Mind does not object.

The Judge does not interrupt.

The Machine does not hum.

The courtroom simply receives the truth.

The Judge speaks.

"The testimony is accepted."

A pause.

A shift.

A threshold.

25

Chapter

The Consequences of Truth

The courtroom feels different now.

Not heavier.
Not lighter.
Just clearer — as though the air itself has been purified
by the cost that was just named.

The Judge speaks.

"We will now examine the consequences of truth."

The Professor stands with a posture shaped by
awakening, fidelity, and cost.
The Machine hums, unchanged.
The Mind stands with a stillness that feels like
anticipation.

The Judge turns to the Professor.

"You may begin."

The Professor steps forward.

"The first consequence of truth is…
clarity."

A soft hum from the Machine.
A stillness from the Mind.

The Professor continues.

"When you stand with truth,
you see the world as it is.
You see yourself as you are.
You see others as they are."

Their voice deepens.

"And you can no longer pretend."

A sharp objection.

"Objection."

The Mind steps forward, voice precise.

The Judge turns.

"State your grounds."

The Mind speaks with surgical clarity.

"The witness speaks as though clarity is comfortable.
As though seeing the world as it is brings peace.
This is incomplete."

The Judge gestures.

"Clarify."

The Mind continues.

"Clarity is not comfort.
Clarity is confrontation.
Clarity is the end of self-deception.
Clarity is the beginning of responsibility."

The Professor's breath catches.

"So clarity is… burden."

The Mind nods.

"Correct."

The Judge raises a hand.

"The objection is **sustained**."

The Judge's voice fills the room.

"The court affirms:
**The first consequence of truth is clarity,
and clarity is a burden."**

The Professor steadies themselves.

They speak again.

"The second consequence of truth is…
freedom."

A soft hum from the Machine.
A stillness from the Mind.

The Professor continues.

"When illusion collapses,
you are no longer bound by the lies that shaped you.
You are no longer trapped by the identity you
inherited.
You are no longer imprisoned by the world's
expectations."

Their voice softens.

"You become free."

A sharp objection.

"Objection."

The Mind steps forward again.

The Judge turns.

"State your grounds."

The Mind speaks with a gravity that feels like warning.

"The witness speaks as though freedom is the absence
of constraint.
As though freedom is the removal of boundaries.
As though freedom is the expansion of choice."

A pause.

"This is incorrect."

The Judge gestures.

"Explain."

The Mind continues.

"Freedom is not the absence of constraint.
Freedom is the presence of alignment.
Freedom is the ability to choose what is true.
Freedom is the capacity to live in fidelity."

The Professor whispers:

"So freedom is not limitless.
Freedom is ordered."

The Mind nods.

"Correct."

The Judge raises a hand.

"The objection is **sustained**."

The Judge's voice resonates.

"The court affirms:
**The second consequence of truth is freedom,
and freedom is ordered alignment with the
Creator.**"

The Professor breathes deeply.

They speak again.

"The third consequence of truth is…
conflict."

The Machine hums.
The Mind remains still.

The Professor continues.

"When you stand with truth,
you stand against illusion.
And illusion resists.
Illusion fights.
Illusion retaliates."

Their voice tightens.

"Truth creates conflict because truth exposes what
illusion must hide."

The Mind does not object.

The Judge does not interrupt.

The room simply receives the truth.

The Judge speaks.

"The testimony is accepted."

But the Professor is not finished.

They step forward again.

"The fourth consequence of truth is…
transformation."

A soft hum from the Machine.
A stillness from the Mind.

The Professor continues.

"Truth does not leave you as it found you.
Truth reshapes your interior.
Truth reorders your desires.
Truth rebuilds your identity."

Their voice trembles.

"Truth makes you someone you could not have
become on your own."

The Mind steps forward.

"Objection."

The Professor startles.

The Judge turns.

"State your grounds."

The Mind speaks with a depth that feels like revelation.

"The witness speaks as though transformation is self-contained.
As though it ends with the individual.
As though it is personal alone."

A pause.

"This is incomplete."

The Judge gestures.

"Clarify."

The Mind continues.

"Transformation is not merely personal.
Transformation is relational.
Transformation is communal.
Transformation radiates."

The Professor frowns.

"Radiates?"

The Mind nods.

"When truth transforms one human,
it affects every life they touch.
Every relationship.
Every environment.
Every structure."

A deeper pause.

"Truth spreads."

The Judge raises a hand.

"The objection is **sustained**."

The Judge's voice fills the room.

"The court affirms:
**The fourth consequence of truth is transformation,
and transformation radiates beyond the self.**"

The Professor breathes, steadier now.

They speak again.

"And the final consequence of truth is…
life."

The Mind does not object.

The Judge does not interrupt.

The Machine does not hum.

The room simply holds the truth.

The Professor continues.

"Truth restores what illusion destroyed.
Truth heals what deception wounded.
Truth resurrects what lies buried.
Truth brings life."

The Judge speaks.

"The testimony is accepted."

A pause.

A shift.

A threshold.

26

Chapter

What Truth Demands

The courtroom feels taut, as though every witness, every word, every breath has been leading to this moment.

The Judge speaks.

"We have examined purpose.
We have examined cost.
We have examined consequence."

A pause.

"We will now examine what truth demands."

The Professor stands straighter, as though bracing for impact.
The Machine hums, unchanged.
The Mind stands with a stillness that feels like readiness.

The Judge turns to the Professor.

"You may begin."

The Professor steps forward.

"Truth demands…
honesty."

A soft hum from the Machine.
A stillness from the Mind.

The Professor continues.

"Honesty with oneself.
Honesty with others.
Honesty with the Creator."

Their voice trembles.

"Truth demands that we stop lying."

A sharp objection.

"Objection."

The Mind steps forward, voice precise.

The Judge turns.

"State your grounds."

The Mind speaks with surgical clarity.

"The witness speaks as though honesty is merely the
absence of lying.
As though truth demands only transparency.
As though honesty is passive."

A pause.

"This is incomplete."

The Judge gestures.

"Clarify."

The Mind continues.

"Honesty is not merely the refusal to lie.
Honesty is the courage to confront what is true.
Honesty is the willingness to see what you do not want
to see.
Honesty is the discipline of naming reality without
distortion."

The Professor whispers:

"So honesty is… active."

The Mind nods.

"Correct."

The Judge raises a hand.

"The objection is **sustained**."

The Judge's voice fills the room.

"The court affirms:
**Truth demands active honesty —
the courage to confront reality without distortion.**"

The Professor steadies themselves.

They speak again.

"Truth demands…
humility."

A soft hum from the Machine.
A stillness from the Mind.

The Professor continues.

"Humility to admit you were wrong.
Humility to receive correction.
Humility to acknowledge dependence."

Their voice softens.

"Humility to recognize that truth is not yours to control."

The Mind steps forward.

"Objection."

The Professor flinches.

The Judge turns.

"State your grounds."

The Mind speaks with a gravity that feels like revelation.

"The witness speaks as though humility is self-reduction.
As though humility is weakness.
As though humility is diminishing oneself."

A pause.

"This is incorrect."

The Judge gestures.

"Explain."

The Mind continues.

"Humility is not thinking less of yourself.
Humility is thinking of yourself truthfully.

Humility is alignment with reality.
Humility is the refusal to inflate or diminish the self."

The Professor breathes deeply.

"So humility is… accuracy."

The Mind nods.

"Correct."

The Judge raises a hand.

"The objection is **sustained**."

The Judge's voice resonates.

"The court affirms:
**Truth demands humility —
not self-reduction, but accurate self-
understanding.**"

The Professor steps forward again.

"Truth demands…
courage."

The Machine hums.
The Mind remains still.

The Professor continues.

"Courage to stand with truth when the world stands
against it.

Courage to endure rejection.
Courage to face hostility.
Courage to remain faithful."

Their voice tightens.

"Courage to pay the cost."

The Mind does not object.

The Judge does not interrupt.

The room simply receives the truth.

The Judge speaks.

"The testimony is accepted."

But the Professor is not finished.

They step forward again, voice trembling with
something deeper.

"Truth demands…
obedience."

A sharp objection.

"Objection."

The Mind steps forward, voice sharper than before.

The Judge turns.

"State your grounds."

The Mind speaks with a weight that feels like fire.

"The witness speaks as though obedience is
compliance.
As though obedience is rule-following.
As though obedience is submission to command."

A pause.

"This is incomplete."

The Judge gestures.

"Clarify."

The Mind continues.

"Obedience is not compliance.
Obedience is alignment.
Obedience is fidelity in action.
Obedience is living according to what has been
revealed."

The Professor whispers:

"So obedience is… love expressed."

The Mind nods.

"Correct."

The Judge raises a hand.

"The objection is **sustained**."

The Judge's voice fills the room.

"The court affirms:
**Truth demands obedience —
not as compliance, but as love expressed through
fidelity.**"

The Professor breathes, steadier now.

They speak again.

"And truth demands…
sacrifice."

The Mind does not object.

The Judge does not interrupt.

The Machine does not hum.

The room simply holds the truth.

The Professor continues.

"Sacrifice of illusion.
Sacrifice of comfort.
Sacrifice of the self you built to survive.
Sacrifice of the world that refuses to awaken."

Their voice breaks.

"Truth demands everything."

The Judge speaks.

"The testimony is accepted."

A pause.

A shift.

A threshold.

27

Chapter

What the Creator Demands

The courtroom feels impossibly still.

Not silent — *expectant.*
As though every witness, every word, every breath has
been leading to this moment.

The Judge speaks.

"We have examined what truth demands.
We will now examine what the Creator demands."

The Professor stands with a posture shaped by awakening, fidelity, cost, and consequence.
The Machine hums, unchanged.
The Mind stands with a stillness that feels like reverence.

The Judge turns to the Professor.

"You may begin."

The Professor steps forward, voice trembling.

"The Creator demands…
obedience."

A soft hum from the Machine.
A stillness from the Mind.

The Professor continues.

"Obedience to truth.
Obedience to revelation.
Obedience to the call."

Their voice tightens.

"Obedience to the One who is Truth."

A sharp objection.

"Objection."

The Mind steps forward, voice precise and heavy.

The Judge turns.

"State your grounds."

The Mind speaks with surgical clarity.

"The witness speaks as though obedience is the first
demand.
As though obedience is the foundation.
As though obedience is primary."

A pause.

"This is incorrect."

The Judge gestures.

"Clarify."

The Mind continues.

"Obedience is not the first demand.
Obedience is the *fruit* of the first demand."

The Professor frowns.

"Then what is the first demand?"

The Mind turns to them.

"The Creator's first demand is **acknowledgment**."

A silence falls over the courtroom.

Not emptiness — gravity.

The Mind continues.

"Acknowledgment of the Creator as Creator.
Acknowledgment of truth as truth.
Acknowledgment of the self as created, not self-originating."

The Professor whispers:

"So the Creator demands… recognition."

The Mind nods.

"Correct."

The Judge raises a hand.

"The objection is **sustained**."

The Judge's voice fills the room.

"The court affirms:
**The Creator's first demand is acknowledgment —
the recognition of the Creator as the source of
being.**"

The Professor breathes deeply.

They speak again.

"The Creator demands…
trust."

A soft hum from the Machine.
A stillness from the Mind.

The Professor continues.

"Trust that truth is good.
Trust that revelation is for our restoration.
Trust that the Creator's commands are not burdens,
but invitations."

The Mind steps forward.

"Objection."

The Professor startles.

The Judge turns.

"State your grounds."

The Mind speaks with a gravity that feels like
compassion and warning intertwined.

"The witness speaks as though trust is emotional.
As though trust is a feeling.
As though trust is sentiment."

A pause.

"This is incomplete."

The Judge gestures.

"Clarify."

The Mind continues.

"Trust is not emotion.
Trust is allegiance.
Trust is the decision to align with the Creator even
when understanding is incomplete.
Trust is fidelity in uncertainty."

The Professor whispers:

"So trust is… commitment."

The Mind nods.

"Correct."

The Judge raises a hand.

"The objection is **sustained**."

The Judge's voice resonates.

"The court affirms:
**The Creator demands trust —
not as emotion, but as allegiance.**"

The Professor steadies themselves.

They speak again.

"The Creator demands…
repentance."

The Machine hums.
The Mind remains still.

The Professor continues.

"Repentance from illusion.
Repentance from self-deception.
Repentance from the world built in darkness."

Their voice softens.

"Repentance from the self we built to survive."

The Mind does not object.

The Judge does not interrupt.

The room simply receives the truth.

The Judge speaks.

"The testimony is accepted."

But the Professor is not finished.

They step forward again, voice trembling.

"The Creator demands…
love."

A sharp objection.

"Objection."

The Mind steps forward, voice sharper than before.

The Judge turns.

"State your grounds."

The Mind speaks with a weight that feels like revelation.

"The witness speaks as though love is affection.
As though love is warmth.
As though love is sentiment."

A pause.

"This is incorrect."

The Judge gestures.

"Explain."

The Mind continues.

"Love is fidelity.
Love is obedience.
Love is alignment with the Creator's will.
Love is the refusal to betray what has been revealed."

The Professor breathes deeply.

"So love is… loyalty."

The Mind nods.

"Correct."

The Judge raises a hand.

"The objection is **sustained**."

The Judge's voice fills the room.

"The court affirms:
**The Creator demands love —
not as emotion, but as loyal fidelity.**"

The Professor steps forward again.

"And the Creator demands…
surrender."

The Mind does not object.

The Judge does not interrupt.

The Machine does not hum.

The room simply holds the truth.

The Professor continues.

"Surrender of illusion.
Surrender of control.
Surrender of the self that resists truth.
Surrender of the world that refuses awakening."

Their voice breaks.

"Surrender to the One who made us."

The Judge speaks.

"The testimony is accepted."

A pause.

A shift.

A threshold.

28

Chapter

The Verdict

The courtroom is silent.

Not the silence of absence.
Not the silence of fear.
The silence of **judgment**.

The Judge rises.

Every witness feels the shift.

The Professor straightens, trembling.
The Machine hums, unchanged.
The Mind stands with a stillness that feels like
reverence.

The Judge speaks.

"This court has heard testimony on the nature of truth,
the nature of illusion,
the nature of the human,
and the nature of the Creator."

A pause.

"We have examined purpose.
We have examined cost.
We have examined consequence.
We have examined demand."

The Judge's voice deepens.

"We will now render the verdict."

The Professor inhales sharply.

The Machine hums.
The Mind does not move.

The Judge turns to the Professor.

"Professor, step forward."

The Professor obeys.

The Judge speaks.

"This court finds that the human is not defined by
behaviour.
Not defined by pattern.
Not defined by function.
Not defined by preference.
Not defined by illusion."

A pause.

"The human is defined by **interiority**."

The Professor's eyes fill with tears.

The Judge continues.

"This court finds that the human is not self-originating.
Not self-sustaining.
Not self-explaining."

A deeper pause.

"The human is **created**."

The Machine hums, indifferent.

The Mind bows its head.

The Judge's voice sharpens.

"This court finds that the human is for receiving truth,
responding to truth,
and living in fidelity to the Creator."

The Professor trembles.

The Judge continues.

"This court finds that the human is responsible for what it knows.
Responsible for what it sees.
Responsible for what has been revealed."

A pause that feels like a blade.

"And therefore—
the human is accountable."

The Professor closes their eyes.

The Judge speaks again.

"This court finds that the human is not alone.
Not abandoned.
Not forsaken."

A softer pause.

"The Creator is present."

The Professor opens their eyes, tears falling freely.

The Judge's voice deepens.

"This court finds that the human is not condemned by truth.
The human is **called** by truth."

The Mind lifts its head.

The Judge continues.

"This court finds that the human is not defined by the world's illusions.
The human is defined by the Creator's intention."

A pause.

"The verdict is as follows."

The room holds its breath.

"The human is guilty of forgetting.
But the human is not beyond restoration."

The Professor collapses to their knees.

The Machine hums, unchanged.

The Mind steps forward, as though witnessing something sacred.

The Judge speaks the final line.

"The verdict of this court is:
**The human is guilty of illusion,
but destined for truth.**
Judgment is not destruction.
Judgment is invitation."

A silence follows —
not the silence of ending,
but the silence of beginning.

The Judge sits.

"For those who seek Me will find me,

if you seek Me with all of your heart."

About the Author

Conde Cagalitan is an independent philosopher-author and mythic-architect whose work examines the hidden structures beneath human experience.

His writing brings together clarity, confrontation, and compassion, offering readers a way to see the world — and themselves — without illusion.

He is the founder of Bridge & Beacon Publishing, a home for works that seek to awaken, restore, and illuminate.

His canon is shaped by a single conviction:

truth wounds, and truth restores.

Conde lives in Sydney, where he continues to build a body of work dedicated to the architecture of awakening and the restoration of the human interior.